Business Fundamentals for Law Students

Business Fundamentals

for

Law Students

Concepts, Problem Sets, and Case Studies

Julie D. Lawton

PROFESSOR OF LAW

DEPAUL UNIVERSITY COLLEGE OF LAW

Carolina Academic Press

DURHAM, NORTH CAROLINA

LIBRARY OF CONGRESS CATALOGING-IN-PUBLICATION DATA

Names: Lawton, Julie D., author.
Title: Business fundamentals for lawyers / by Julie D. Lawton.
Description: Durham, North Carolina : Carolina Academic Press, LLC, [2023]
Identifiers: LCCN 2022060249 (print) | LCCN 2022060250 (ebook) |
    ISBN 9781531019969 (paperback) | ISBN 9781531019976 (ebook)
Subjects: LCSH: Business enterprises--Law and legislation--United States. |
    Financial statements--Law and legislation--United States. | LCGFT: Textbooks.
Classification: LCC KF1355 .L38 2023 (print) | LCC KF1355 (ebook) |
    DDC 346.73/065--dc23/eng/20230403
LC record available at https://lccn.loc.gov/2022060249
LC ebook record available at https://lccn.loc.gov/2022060250

Carolina Academic Press
700 Kent Street
Durham, North Carolina 27701
(919) 489-7486
www.cap-press.com

Printed in the United States of America

Contents

Introduction

This book is designed to assist law students, particularly those planning to practice business law, learning the basics of business. In addition to narrative explanations of business concepts, unlike most other books on this subject, this book also will provide case studies and problem sets to enable law students to experientially learn how to identify legal issues from analyzing business issues to analyzing financial statements. In this book, we will use a fictional company, Widget Shoes, as an evolving example to help explore the concepts covered.

Accountants, not lawyers, create financial statements, so it is important to understand that the purpose of this book is not to teach the law student how to draft financial statements. Instead, the purpose is to help the law student develop a sufficient understanding of business concepts to be able to function as an attorney in a business environment, whether in business law or in litigation.

After teaching Business Fundamentals for Law Students and Accounting for Lawyers for several years, I find many law students who are new to business concepts struggle with these concepts as it is often akin to a foreign language. For law students new to business concepts, a book such as this that focuses on fundamentals is a more effective teaching tool that one covering the more complex and theoretical business concepts that most business lawyers will never use.

Ideally in a Business Fundamentals for Law Students course, students should finish the course with an ability to read and analyze the four main financial statements, understand time value of money, understand the business perspective of debt and equity and their roles in the financial markets, and have the ability to use those tools to identify legal risks and means of mitigating those risks on behalf of their clients. While this skill is useful to all law students and lawyers, it is particularly vital to future business lawyers.

For their review, comments, and input many thanks to the participants in the 2019 NYU Clinical Writers Workshop (Profs. Susan Bennett, Ted DeBarbieri, Amanda Spratley, and Bernice Grant). Additional thanks to attorney and friend Markena Peavy, and attorney and friend Steven Wiser. For research assistance, many thanks to Anthony McCloud, II and Iqra Mushtaq. A very special thanks to Zach Prociuk whose tireless research assistance contributed greatly to the completion of this book. Thank you to our amazing library colleagues at DePaul University College of Law for invaluable assistance in drafting this book. And, of course, my very patient editor who helped nurture this book from a very early draft to completion.

I am my ancestors' wildest dreams.

- To my ancestral family, on whose shoulders and in whose shadows I stand, I honor and thank you.
- To my parents whose love continues to inspire me.
- To my big sister who has always given me the space to shine.
- To my darling husband, I thank you for loving the me that I love.

Business Fundamentals for Law Students

One

Overview of the Business Structure

A. Why Should I Care?

Since you are currently and assuredly happily taking this course, presumably you have already thought about this question, but for those of you still on the fence with the date of the last day of Add/Drop tantalizingly in the back of your mind, consider the following:

1. Business Fundamentals in Family Law

Your client, a soon-to-be ex-husband, is in final negotiations with his soon-to-be ex-wife about alimony payments as part of the divorce settlement. Her attorney, your opposing counsel, makes a settlement offer of either (i) $800,000 lump sum payment now or $200,000 annually over the next five years. How do you know how to advise your client if you do not yet understand the concept of time value of money where a dollar today is worth more than a dollar tomorrow? How do you determine which offer is the most financially advantageous? Some of you may think that you'll just hire a business consultant to calculate these terms for you. As an initial matter, that is an additional expense. Additionally, and more importantly, if you do not understand the concept, how do you then explain the calculated results to your client to enable your client to make an informed decision?

2. Business Fundamentals in Personal Injury Law

Your client was injured in a car accident and has been out of work for the past 4 months. He anticipates that he will not be able to work again for another 6 months, and even then, he will only be able to work part-time until his injuries are completely healed. You are negotiating a settlement for your client with the other driver's insurance company. As part of preparing a settlement demand, you begin to calculate your client's expenses and losses. You certainly know to demand the lost wages from being out of work for the past 4 months, but how do you calculate the future lost wages? Do you simply project what your client would have been paid? If so, how do you account for the time value of money where a dollar today is worth more than a dollar tomorrow? How do you calculate the financial loss he has incurred by no longer being able to contribute to his 401k retirement plan? If his 401k contributions would have been invested in a mutual fund earning 8%, how do you calculate what his lost investment earnings would have been? Again, even if you hire a business consultant to calculate these terms, how do you, as the attorney, defend the demand in the negotiations if you do not understand the underlying concepts?

3. Business Fundamentals for the Solo Practitioner

You have graduated law school full of knowledge, optimism and, yes, tuition loans. You decide to open your own firm and as we like to say "hang your shingle." You find a wonderful small office space in the growing city of Columbus, OH and meet with the landlord to negotiate terms. The landlord agrees to reduce the monthly rent if you agree to renovate the space to your needs. No problem, you muse, as you begin to envision the eager clients who will soon line up outside your office door. You meet with a contractor to complete the build-out of your new office space, and the contractor informs you that the renovations will cost $10,000. Without needing to check your bank account, you know that you do not have that much cash, so you decide to meet with lenders to obtain a loan. You talk with one lender who says it will extend the loan to you with a $10,000 principal, a 5-year term, a 1% underwriting fee, and an 8% interest rate. That sounds like a reasonable option until you hear from another lender who offers you a loan with $10,000 principal, a 3-year term, a 1.5% underwriting fee and a 6% interest rate. Which loan is the most financially advantageous for you? What is the total cost of all of the charges? And, you're probably wondering, what, pray tell, is an underwriting fee?

4. Business Fundamentals in Intellectual Property Litigation

You have graduated from law school (finally!) and join this fantastic local boutique law firm specializing in IP litigation. Your firm represents a group of women who formed a business which is applying for a patent for their new running shoe that increases caloric burn by 20%. One of the largest shoe companies, who like all companies just loves competition, instead of welcoming this new competitor to the marketplace, contacts your clients offering to purchase the patent for the shoe. Your client asks you to lead the negotiations, as they are engineers, not IP lawyers. The company submits an offer to your clients that offers a price contingent on successfully obtaining the patent and based on the discounted cash flow from the anticipated future stream of cash flow from the sale of this high-calorie-burn shoe. The client's business consultants send the term sheet to you that

> **Definition**
>
> *Term Sheet*
>
> Term Sheets refer to the document containing the business terms of a transaction that are agreed to before drafting a contract memorializing the transaction.

includes provisions that will need to be included in the IP Sales Agreement including minimum revenue generation, minimum internal rate of return requirements, and minimum gross profit margins. The term sheet also details the IP purchase terms, including that the owners' payment will be partially in cash and partially in the acquiring company's common stock that will vest over time.

Some of this confusing to you? You're in the right place—let's begin.

B. Corporations Overview

As you will soon learn, corporations use financial statements to display, in a recognizable and consistent format, the corporation's financial condition and its financial performance as of the end of the corporation's operating cycle, known as a corporation's "fiscal period." While some of you may have studied the corporate structure before enrolling in this course, others may not; so, before delving too deeply into the business concepts, this section will provide a very quick overview of the corporate structure.

You probably have heard the term "limited liability" in your law school career. With some notable exceptions, creating a corporation, or incorporating, limits the amount of capital that owners, known as shareholders, can lose when a corporation is subject to liability. For example, if a corporation is subjected to liability because of a lawsuit, the question arises about how to satisfy that judgment. The first source to satisfy the judgment is for the judgment to be paid with the corporation's cash or its other items of value that can be sold for cash. However, what if that amount is insufficient? How would the judgment be satisfied? The natural thought is to try to attach, or somehow obtain, the personal assets of the owners of the corporation. To protect against that risk, individuals often form corporations, which provide protection against the owners' personal assets being used to satisfy debts of the corporation. Simply, a corporation is a business entity formed pursuant to state statute that, upon creation, becomes a separate legal entity from the individual and will be regulated by the relevant state's corporations or business organizations statute. This limited liability is a major benefit of creating a corporation. The concept of limited liability protects an owner's personal assets from being taken to satisfy the liabilities of the corporation.[1] Generally, a corporate owner's capital loss is limited to the amount of capital that the shareholder invested in the corporation, either by loaning capital to the corporation or by purchasing units of ownership, or shares, in the corporation.

---

1. There are exceptions involving fraud or intentionally under-capitalizing the corporation that are more fully covered in a law school course on corporations or business organizations.

C. Creating the Corporation

To create a corporation, a lawyer would consult the state corporations statute where the corporation will be incorporated. To form a corporation, individuals[2] would complete the filing requirements set forth in the state corporations statute. These requirements may vary, but generally involve completing the corporation's document of creation, the Articles of Incorporation, and filing those Articles of Incorporation with the state's Secretary of State or other relevant government agency. Articles of Incorporation contain a number of items such as (i) the name of the corporation, (ii) the purpose for which the corporation is organized, (iii) the address of the corporation's initial office, (iv) the name and address of each Incorporator (the persons organizing the corporation), and (v) information about the number and classes of shares the corporation is authorized and proposes to issue.

Once the corporation is formed, the corporation can issue shares of the corporation to investors who, by purchasing shares, become shareholders.[3] Generally, a corporation issues some variation of two types of shares—common stock and preferred stock.[4]

D. Corporate Purpose

What is the purpose of a corporation? On the surface, it is easy to argue that a for-profit corporation's purpose is that purpose set forth in the corporation's Articles of Incorporation. But it's not quite that simple, is it? For many entrepreneurs, the corporation's purpose is to operate its day-to-day business in a way that generates a profit for the business' owners. However, should self-directed profit earning be the sole or primary purpose of a business? Or should a business' operations also consider the business' impact on the broader society? To help you consider this, let us review an originalist view of corporate purpose from 1970 and contrast that with an alternative view from 2019.

On September 13, 1970, noted economist Milton Friedman published "A Friedman doctrine—The Social Responsibility Of Business Is to Increase Its Profits" in the New York Times.[5] In this article, Dr. Friedman famously argued that in "a free-enterprise, private-property system, a corporate executive is an employee of the owners," or shareholders, of the corporation.[6] According to Dr. Friedman, a corpo-

---

2. Corporations can be formed by individuals or other corporations.

3. There are rules governing the sale of securities, such as shares of a corporation, that will not be discussed here but are covered in detail in a law school course on Securities Regulations.

4. For more detail about common stock and preferred stock, see our chapters on the Balance Sheet, Debt Analysis, and Equity Analysis.

5. https://www.nytimes.com/1970/09/13/archives/a-friedman-doctrine-the-social-responsibility-of-business-is-to.html.

6. *Id.*

rate executive has "direct responsibility to his [or her] employers," more than a direct responsibility to the greater social good.[7] Dr. Friedman posited the corporate executive's responsibility is to conduct the business in accordance with the shareholders' desires, "which generally will be to make as much money as possible while conforming to the basic rules of the society, both those embodied in law and those embodied in ethical custom."[8]

He argues that "[t]he whole justification for permitting the corporate executive to be selected by the stockholders is that the executive is an agent serving the interests of his [or her] principal. This justification disappears when the corporate executive imposes taxes and spends the proceeds for 'social' purposes."[9]

He concludes—

That is why...I have called it a "fundamentally subversive doctrine" in a free society, and have said that in such a society, "there is one and only one social responsibility of business—to use its resources and engage in activities designed to increase its profits so long as it stays within the rules of the game, which is to say, engages in open and free competition without deception fraud.[10]

Contrast that with a statement released on August 19, 2019, from the Business Roundtable, an association of chief executive officers of leading American companies. With this new statement, the Corporate Roundtable superseded its previous statements endorsing "principles of shareholder primacy" with its new statement endorsing "a modern standard for corporate responsibility."[11] According to the statement, this modern standard of corporate responsibility includes commitments to paying their employees fair compensation, and supporting their neighboring communities with a commitment to "respect the people in our communities and protect the environment by embracing sustainable practices across our businesses."[12] Many of you will have corporations as clients. What do you think should be the purpose of a corporation? Should it have the singular self-serving purpose espoused by Dr. Friedman, the broader societal responsibility set forth by the Corporate Roundtable, or do you think corporations have an even greater responsibility to the communities in which they operate?

---

7. *Id.*
8. *Id.*
9. *Id.*
10. Id.
11. https://www.businessroundtable.org/business-roundtable-redefines-the-purpose-of-a
-corporation-to-promote-an-economy-that-serves-all-americans.
12. *Id.*

E. Corporation Management

After a corporation is formed, the corporation must determine how it will operate on a daily basis. To accomplish this, the corporation will adopt a set of rules and regulations, called By-laws, that set forth how the corporation will self-govern. Generally, the By-laws will contain provisions for the regulation and management of the affairs of the corporation consistent with federal and state law and the Articles of Incorporation.

As shown in the chart below, while the corporation is owned by shareholders, the broad direction and policy of the corporation is set by a Board of Directors—individuals who, as set forth in the state's corporations statute, are elected by shareholders. The Board of Directors, in turn, are generally empowered to hire and fire the officers of the corporation. Finally, the officers are empowered to hire and fire the non-officer employees.

Overall, the corporate management structure looks something like this:

This hierarchy makes the Board of Directors, as managers of the corporation, accountable to the shareholders, the owners of the corporation. However, there are times when a corporation's structure inhibits this hierarchy—see the case study on Facebook below.

Case Study 1.1—Facebook Shareholders Seek Better Oversight

Your corporate client is a shareholder in Facebook. Imagine that your client tells you that, as one of Facebook's shareholders, the client wants new Directors on the Board and that the client wants to push for changes with the corporation's Chief Executive Officer ("CEO").

As you now know, shareholders elect the Board of Directors, and the Board of Director hires the corporation's officers.

You, a newly minted business lawyer, recall from your studies in law school and your review of corporate law that shareholders have the right to vote for or against Directors at the annual meeting of shareholders, and this right generally makes Directors and officers, including the CEO, accountable to the shareholders. Consider what happens when the corporate structure minimizes this accountability because the CEO has shares that provide the CEO with a greater voting block than the other shareholders. How do shareholders hold the Board of Directors and, hence the CEO, accountable to the shareholders if the shareholder voting block is insufficient to outvote the CEO?

To help you consider this question, review the proposal brought by NorthStar Asset Management, Inc. of Boston ("NorthStar"), which in 2015 was a shareholder of Facebook, one of the country's largest companies. According to NorthStar, "[i]n 2015, one of Facebook's shareholders, NorthStar Asset Management, Inc. of Boston, began addressing this dilemma by submitting a proposal at the annual meeting of Facebook's shareholders, building off of a proposal filed in 2014 by individual shareholder and corporate governance advocate James McRitchie, in an attempt to limit this structure and to decrease the voting power of the CEO. According to NorthStar, after receiving significant shareholder support, NorthStar has re-filed that proposal annually since that time."[13]

Read the press release, proposal and commentary below to better understand how the law was used to create a corporate structure that impacts the control shareholders can exercise over the Board of Directors, and by extension, the CEO.

---

13. Email from Lizzie Sanderson, the Client Services Coordinator, for NorthStar Asset Management, Inc. sent on January 2, 2020, to Author.

NorthStar's Press Release:[14]

Posted By: Mari Schwartzer
Date: May 23, 2019
Facebook Shareholders Seek Better Oversight

Boston, MA (May 23, 2019)—Amid company controversy, shareholders at the May 30th Facebook annual meeting will ask that Mark Zuckerberg hand over his oversized control of the company and create a governance structure allowing all shareholders one vote per share.

At Facebook, two shares of stock exist—ordinary shares with one vote (class A), and insider shares with 10 votes per share (class B). Critics of dual-class voting structures point out that it would be essentially impossible for class A shareholders to "outvote" the founders, even on significant or concerning matters. NorthStar's shareholder proposal asks the board to "take all practicable steps in its control to initiate and adopt a recapitalization plan for all outstanding stock to have one vote per share."

The proposal, brought by NorthStar Asset Management, Inc. of Boston, received an estimated support of 81% of outsider class A shareholders at the 2018 annual meeting.

"We've brought this proposal year after year because the source of Facebook's poor corporate governance is the share structure. Shareholders and the Board are powerless due to Zuckerberg's outsized voting rights," explained NorthStar Asset Management, Inc., CEO Julie Goodridge.

"Through these shareholder resolutions each year, common shareholders have repeatedly shown concern regarding management's super-voting rights, and this year's proposal is timely given the seemingly endless string of issues at Facebook," stated NorthStar's Director of Shareholder Activism and Engagement, Mari Schwartzer.

NorthStar argues that the controversies following Facebook are rooted in how insulated from criticism the CEO and board have become thanks to the dual-class share structure. "The company has faced serious allegations—from data privacy scandals to being implicated in human rights abuses in Myanmar and India—but shareholders have no way to address controversy through their voting rights. This puts our investment at risk," continued Goodridge. "Critics are calling for the company to be split up or for Zuckerberg to step down. Yet if he did resign, shareholders would suddenly be faced with a disgruntled founder with majority voting power—and that could be dangerous for the company."

---

14. Reprinted with permission from NorthStar Asset Management. Permission on file.

NorthStar has filed a voluntary exempt solicitation with the SEC to urge shareholder support....

NorthStar Asset Management, Inc., is a wealth management company based in Boston with a focus on socially responsible investing. At NorthStar, creative shareholder engagement is a positive force for change.

Here is NorthStar's Shareholder Rebuttal regarding its 2018 Shareholder Proposal.[15]

Shareholder Rebuttal to Facebook, Inc. Opposition Statement Regarding Equal Voting Rights

240.14a-103 Notice of Exempt Solicitation
U.S. Securities and Exchange Commission, Washington DC 20549

NAME OF REGISTRANT: Facebook, Inc.

NAME OF PERSON RELYING ON EXEMPTION: NorthStar Asset Management, Inc.

ADDRESS OF PERSON RELYING ON EXEMPTION: 2 Harris Avenue, Boston MA 02130

Written materials are submitted pursuant to Rule 14a-6(g)(1) promulgated under the Securities Exchange Act of 1934.*

*Submission is not required of this filer under the terms of the Rule, but is made voluntarily in the interest of public disclosure and consideration of these important issues.

Facebook shareowners are encouraged to vote <u>FOR</u> proposal #3:

Resolved: Shareholders request that our Board take all practicable steps in its control toward initiating and adopting a recapitalization plan for all outstanding stock to have one vote per share. This would include efforts at the earliest practicable time toward encouragement and negotiation with Class B shareholders to request that they relinquish, for the common good of all shareholders, any pre-existing disproportionate rights. This is not intended to unnecessarily limit our Board's judgment in crafting the requested change in accordance with applicable laws and existing contracts.

continued

15. Copyright license on file with author.

continued

Overview

Recently, Facebook has been thrust into news headlines repeatedly for controversies that investors and Facebook users find quite troubling. In the past two months alone, our Company has been characterized by headlines such as:

"Facebook says the number of users affected by Cambridge Analytica data leak is 87 million" (CNBC; 4/4/18)

"Facebook Wasn't 'Forthcoming' With Congress, Senator Says" (Bloomberg; 3/26/18)

"Facebook sent a doctor on a secret mission to ask hospitals to share patient data" (CNBC; 4/5/18)

"Facebook's facial recognition violates user privacy, watchdog groups plan to tell FTC" (USA Today; 4/5/18)

"Zuckerberg Says Facebook Probe Into Apps Won't Uncover All Data Abuse" (Wall Street Journal; 3/22/18)

"Facebook has lost $80 billion in market value since its data scandal" (CNN Money; 3/27/18)

The Proponent believes that these recent incidents clearly illustrate the need for shareholders to have the opportunity to participate in decision-making at our Company. In the opinion of the Proponent, the current share structure affords the shareholders who put capital at risk since the Company went public **absolutely no consequential manner of communicating dissent** with any decision Mr. Zuckerberg makes. In light of recent scandals in particular, the Proponent believes that equal voting is one crucial mechanism needed to safeguard future loss of shareholder value.

Management and board decisions are putting shareholder value at risk, without shareholder recourse against Mr. Zuckerberg or the Board.

Shareholders that have invested in Facebook since its inception, providing billions of dollars of capital for the Company to grow, and the Proponent believes that those common shareholders now face the greatest risk of loss in the face of poor decision-making by Mr. Zuckerberg and the board of directors.

Shareholders bought into Facebook's mission and strategy, but the Proponent believes that recent events have shown that Management is not upholding the Company mission as intended. In direct contrast to the Company's opposition statement that declares that "we are focused on our mission of giving people the power to build community and bring the world closer together," in the opinion of the Proponent, our Company's recent actions and strategies have served to create a more divisive world, completely contrary to our Company mission and goal.

The same opposition statement also asserts that "If we focus on this mission and build useful and engaging products and services, we believe we will create the most value for our stockholders over the long term. Our board of directors believes that our capital structure contributes to our stability and **insulates our board of directors and management from short-term pressures**, which allows them to focus on our mission and long-term success." [emphasis added] The Proponent contends that the recent scandals emphasize the misguided nature of statement. As our board of directors and management have been insulated from shareholder concerns, shareholder value has been diminished.

Voting at annual elections is a vital safeguard of shareholder value, yet our Company's share structure puts shareholders at risk.

The Securities and Exchange Commission (SEC) tells all shareholders to vote in the annual elections of the companies in which they are invested because "shareholder voting rights give you the power to elect directors at annual or special meetings and make your views known to the company management and directors on significant issues that may affect the value of your shares."[16] **However, at our Company, the shareholders who own the most stock (outsiders) have no say in the issues affecting the Company.** Because insiders with "super-voting shares" (class B) get 10 votes per share, the Proponent believes that it is impossible for class A shareholders to ever vote down a Company-sponsored resolution, including voting down board members that Class A shareholders deem unfit for the board. The Proponent is concerned that without shareholder input that is effective through the annual voting process, the Company may make serious missteps that could have been avoided through equal voting rights.

Research indicates that our Company's voting structure is bad for business.

A comprehensive study, *Incentives vs. Control: An Analysis of U.S. Dual-Class Companies*, concluded that "**the more control that the insiders have, the more they can pursue strategies that are at the expense of outside shareholders**"[17] (emphasis added). The authors found that ceding voting control to insiders—that is, managers unchecked by shareholder input—leads to poor performance over the long-term; even while creating incentives by rewarding

---

16. https://www.sec.gov/investor/pubs/sec-guide-to-proxy-brochures.pdf.

17. "The Effects of Dual-class Ownership on Ordinary Shareholders." Knowledge@Wharton. 30 June 2004. http://knowledge.wharton.upenn.edu/article/the-effects-of-dual-class-ownership-on-ordinary-shareholders/.

continued

continued

managers for their good efforts with greater value through stock ownership leads them to make better decisions. Based upon this research, the Proponent feels that shareholder value is best derived when insider voting control of the firm is separated from insider economic ownership, which has its own reward when stock prices rise.

A study sponsored by the Investor Responsibility Research Center Institute (IRRCi) has shown that on average and over time, companies with multiclass capital structures **underperform** those with a one-share, one-vote standard in which owners' economic risk is commensurate with voting power. This IRRCi study also found that over the long term, controlled companies with a one-share, one-vote structure tend to outperform all others.[18]

Facebook claims that "our success is due in large part to the leadership of our founder and CEO, Mark Zuckerberg, whose vision has guided us from our inception" and that "our board of directors believes that Mr. Zuckerberg has been, and will continue to be, a crucial part of our long-term success." As fiduciaries, the Proponent certainly hopes that Mr. Zuckerberg will continue to be a crucial part of Facebook's long-term success; however, we believe that recent events demonstrate that the use of insider control at Facebook to insulate management from addressing shareholder issues and concerns can have a negative impact on long-term shareholder value. The Proponent wonders, what will happen if the Facebook board decides that the current CEO is incapable of adequately addressing user privacy or content management challenges. Would Mr. Zuckerberg step down if he was asked? And, if so, would the board and/or shareholders be comfortable with having the former founder and minority shareholder by market value continue to exercise majority voting control of the firm?

The Proponent feels that the 2016 approval of a non-voting class of stock further illustrates the Company's disregard for shareholders.

At the 2016 annual meeting of shareholders, the vast majority of outside shareholders voted AGAINST the creation of the non-voting class of stock, however Mr. Zuckerberg and other insiders "voted in" the creation of the non-voting class. The Proponent's calculations indicate that 71% of class A shareholders voted AGAINST the creation of a third, non-voting class of stock.

Despite this overwhelming dissent from shareholders, the non-voting class of stock was approved because class A shareholders cannot outvote Mr. Zuckerberg and other class B holders. The Proponent believes that the heat of shareholder discontent on this issue was demonstrated by the fact that shareholder litigation against the non-voting class of stock eventually moti-

---

18. http://irrcinstitute.org/pdf/FINAL-Controlled-Company-ISS-Report.pdf.

vated Facebook to drop the pursuit of the new class of stock. In the opinion of the Proponent, the intended change to the voting structure was a blatant and obvious attempt to keep control of the Company firmly in Mr. Zuckerberg's hands, giving him full reign to completely disregard risks to shareholder value. Reuters agreed that "Facebook plans new non-voting shares to keep Zuckerberg at helm."[19] Non-insider shareholders already suffer with only 1/10th the voting power of insiders, and the Proponent believes that if Facebook had been able to create a non-voting class of stock, any semblance of opportunity for meaningful engagement with the Company would have been eliminated. Due to the current voting structure, there was no way for common (class A) shareholders to successfully vote against the creation of this non-voting stock.

Without equal shareholder voting, the Proponent is concerned that shareholders will never be able to stop further dilution of their share value, as well as voting rights.

Past performance of this Proposal, in the Proponent's opinion, illustrates shareholder support of equal voting.

The fact that this Proposal has received high votes at each annual meeting, regardless of the fact that Mr. Zuckerberg and other insiders controlled over 50% of the vote each time, illustrates class A stockholders' support of equal shareholder voting. According to the Proponent's calculations, class A shareholders supported this proposal in 2017 with a 61% of the vote in favor (although they were outvoted by the class B super shares held by insiders, of course).

The Proponent believes that the claims by the Company which state that "our stockholders rejected a substantially similar proposal at each of our last four annual meetings of our stockholders," when Mr. Zuckerberg alone controls more than half of the votes due to the dual voting share structure of the firm, **illustrate the problem with the current voting structure.** Despite that fact that shareholders own the majority of the firm, any resolution that Mr. Zuckerberg votes against will fail, regardless of ownership vote. The Proponent feels that without a tally of one-vote-per-share, claiming that stockholders rejected a proposal means little more than Mr. Zuckerberg voted against it.

Despite this robust shareholder support for this proposal and dissent for a non-voting class, the Proponent believes that **Facebook's pursuit of issuing non-voting shares despite clear disapproval from class A shareholders shows blatant disregard for shareholders' rights.**

---

19. https://www.reuters.com/article/us-facebook-results-stock/facebook-plans-new-non-voting-shares-to-keep-zuckerberg-at-helm-idUSKCN0XO2RG.

continued

continued

<u>The Proponent believes that the current dual-class structure is NOT in the best long-term interest of our stockholders and the current corporate governance structure is NOT sound and effective.</u>

The Proponent feels that the current dual-class structure eliminates shareholder checks and balances over Management decisions, and that the recent scandals illustrate the crucial need for the request made in this Proposal. At companies over the long-term, insider control has been shown to sacrifice performance. In his analysis of the nature of economic vs. voting ownership of executives, Wharton professor Andrew Metrick concluded that "sales growth improved as insiders' financial stakes grew, and worsened as they gained voting clout."[20] In other words, disproportional voting rights (wherein insiders have more than one vote per share) can be detrimental to a corporation's bottom line. And as others point out, "[w]ith few constraints placed upon them, managers holding super-class stock can spin out of control. Families and senior managers can entrench themselves into the operations of the company, regardless of their abilities and performance. Finally, dual-class structures may allow management to make bad decisions with few consequences."[21]

Conclusion:

The Proponent believes that this proposal is in the best interest of the company—that it is protective of shareholder value without being overly prescriptive or burdensome. The Proponent also believes that, contrary to Company claims, Facebook's multi-class share structure are not in the best interest of the company or shareholders.

We urge you to vote "FOR" proxy item #3. Should you have any proposal-specific questions please feel free to contact us at mschwartzer@northstarasset.com.

Date: May 17, 2018

By: /s/ Julie N.W. Goodridge

Julie N.W. Goodridge

President & CEO*

NorthStar Asset Management, Inc.

*Julie Goodridge is also the trustee of the NorthStar Asset Management, Inc Funded Pension Plan, one of the proponents.

---

20. http://knowledge.wharton.upenn.edu/article/the-effects-of-dual-class-ownership-on-ordinary-shareholders/.

21. http://www.investopedia.com/articles/fundamental/04/092204.asp#ixzz3X IMQvxdg.

Now that you have reviewed the case study, you should have a better understanding of the role of shareholders and the importance of the share structure in corporate governance. We discuss shares and the statutory rights of shareholders later in the book, so think back on this case study when you study our chapter on Equity Analysis.

F. Why Financial Statements?

Let us consider a hypothetical to introduce you to financial statements. Two of your friends design an amazing running shoe. Since you are a newly minted lawyer, you agree to advise them and begin to think through the legal issues. First, you realize that to make the shoe, they will need to have purchasing contracts with vendors to supply the materials to make the shoe. You also remind them that to sell the shoes, they will need to have either a brick-and-mortar storefront or a digital platform to display the shoes and receive and fulfill shoe orders. If there is a storefront, you know that your friends will need to have a lease with the landlord for the premises. If they use a digital platform, you also know they will need to have a contract with an Internet Service Provider, a payment application, and a website designer. After what surely felt like a long lifetime in law school, you know that a party to a contract has legal liability for that contract, so you are understandably concerned about your friends' personal legal liability for the production, sale, and use of these amazing running shoes. To protect your friends against this personal legal liability, you advise your friends to form a corporation.

You research state laws governing the formation of a corporation in the state where your friends will operate. You then help them complete the requisite forms to create the corporation, Widget Shoes, and remind them to pay the requisite fee. Finally, they receive formal notice from the state that their corporation is formed and has permission to operate. Congratulations! You all are justifiably thrilled!

Widget Shoes, now a duly formed corporation, is ready for business. In your excitement, you think through what to do first. As a well-trained lawyer, you first read through, thoroughly, the corporations statute for the state where Widget Shoes operates. The corporations statute notes that the business and affairs of the corporation shall be managed by, or under, the direction of a Board of Directors. Since the co-founders are the owners and shareholders of the corporation, you advise the Widget Shoes co-founders to select and then elect individuals to serve as members of the Board. Once the Board is elected, the Board selects the officers of the corporation—one friend is selected to serve as President and the other as Vice-President. You and the co-founders now decide the corporation is ready to formally begin operations.

To sell these amazing shoes, the corporation needs some place to manufacture the shoes, such as a factory or a warehouse. The corporate officers identify an ideal location in a manufacturing district and notify the property's landlord of the corporation's interest in leasing the space. The landlord also expresses interest in leasing the space to Widget Shoes but requires both first and last month's rent to sign the lease. The officers also intend to lease equipment to manufacture the shoes, as well as to hire a couple of employees to help with the business. The landlord requires cash for rent, the corporation leasing equipment to Widget Shoes requires an initial cash payment, and the employees require salaries. Your friends elect to invest their hard-earned money to provide initial cash capital to the business in exchange for partial ownership of the business to facilitate the corporation beginning its operations. However, how will the corporation track how much cash was invested in the business? How will the corporation track how much money it is spending to operate? How does it track how much income it is generating? How does the corporation determine whether it is generating sufficient income to cover its expenses? If the corporation does not generate a profit at the end of the corporation's fiscal period, how does the corporation determine why there was not a profit—was it because the corporation did not sell enough shoes or was it because the corporation did not charge a high enough price for each shoe sold? Maybe the corporation spent too much money on operating the business, such as the amount it paid for rent, utilities or salaries?

At a very basic level, these are the purposes of financial statements: to record every financial transaction of a corporation and report these transactions in a consistent format. This format allows financial statement users to review and analyze the corporation's financial condition, including its sales, expenses, cash flow, profitability or liquidity. Lawyers, one group of many users of financial statements, use financial statements to help us identify potential legal issues and manage known legal risks to help our clients mitigate their legal liabilities. Every financial transaction of the corporation, from paying salaries to employees to remitting corporate profits to the corporation's owners, must be recorded in the corporation's financial records to be reflected in the corporation's financial statements.

We will revisit Widget Shoes many times throughout the book as an example of the concepts we will cover.

1. Financial Accounting Foundation and Generally Accepted Accounting Principles

This section provides an explanation of the rules governing accounting and the creation of financial statements. Please note this section is designed as background to provide context for understanding financial statements.

While financial statements are drafted by a corporation's accounting firm or in-house accountant, there are common standards used to govern how accountants record a corporation's financial transactions and how accountants prepare and present financial statements. Broadly, these standards are known as the Generally Accepted Accounting Principles, commonly referred to as GAAP (pronounced "gap") and are drafted, managed and published by the Financial Accounting Foundation ("FAF").

According to the FAF, FAF is an "independent, private-sector, not-for-profit organization ... responsible for the oversight, administration, financing, and appointment of the Financial Accounting Standards Board ("FASB") and the Governmental Accounting Standards Board ("GASB")." The FASB establishes financial accounting and reporting standards for public and private companies and not-for-profit organizations.[22] Further, "the FASB is recognized by the Securities and Exchange Commission as the designated accounting standard setter for public companies."[23] The GASB "establishes accounting and financial reporting standards for U.S. state and local governments...."[24] These two Boards draft and compile the standards which are known collectively as GAAP.

According to the FAF, "GAAP is based on established concepts, objectives, standards, and conventions that have evolved over time to guide how financial statements are prepared and presented. For corporations or not-for-profits, GAAP is set with the objective of providing information that is useful to investors, lenders, or others that provide or may potentially provide resources."[25]

The FAF states that GAAP includes principles on:[26]

- Recognition—what items should be recognized in the financial statements (for example as assets, liabilities, revenues, and expenses).
- Measurement—what amounts should be reported for each of the elements included in financial statements.
- Presentation—what line items, subtotals and totals should be displayed in the financial statements and how might items be aggregated within the financial statements.
- Disclosure—what specific information is most important to the users of the financial statements. Disclosures both supplement and explain amounts in the statements.

Accountants, using GAAP as a guide, will record, categorize, and report a corporation's financial transactions in summarized forms that are commonly referred to as financial statements. There are different types of financial statements. The four major financial statements are: the Balance Sheet, the Income Statement, the Cash

---

22. https://www.accountingfoundation.org/jsp/Foundation/Page/FAFBridgePage&cid =1176164538898, last visited on September 30, 2022.

23. *Id.*

24. *Id.*

25. https://www.accountingfoundation.org/page/PageContent?pageId=/overview-accounting -and-standards/gaap/aboutgaap.html

26. *Id.*

Flow Statement, and the Statement of Stockholder's Equity. These financial statements are a vital means through which corporations provide their financial reporting of the corporation's financial condition and the financial results of the corporation's operations.

Following GAAP's guidance, accountants will summarize all of a corporation's financial transactions into different categories and subcategories on the financial statements. Those categories and subcategories are generally referred to as "Accounts." Accounts, which are displayed as line items on a financial statement, will help you as the user easily determine the end or cumulative balance for the individual accounts as of the date of the financial statement.

2. Financial Statement Publication Intervals

Financial statements are generally produced at regular intervals—monthly, quarterly or, at a minimum, annually. The period of time covered by the financial statement is generally referred to as the fiscal period, or if it is the annual operating period, then it would be referred to as the fiscal year. Barron's Dictionary of Finance and Investment Terms defines fiscal year as an "accounting period covering 12 consecutive months, 52 consecutive weeks, 13 four-week periods, or 365 consecutive days"[27] at the end of which a corporation's accountants will produce financial statements reflecting the corporation's financial position and the results of the corporation's operations as of the end of that fiscal year. It is important to note that for many corporations, their fiscal year coincides with the U.S. calendar year. However, some corporations, such as universities and seasonal corporations, have a fiscal year that does not coincide with the calendar year. In other words, many companies' fiscal years end on December 31 to mirror the US calendar year. Other organizations have fiscal years that coincide with the organization's operating cycle. For example, many colleges and universities have fiscal years that end at the end of June, the end of the college and university academic year which marks the end of the university's operating cycle.

G. Financial Statements Overview

As we have previously discussed, corporations record and present every financial transaction of the corporation on financial statements. For large, public corporations, these financial statements are generally separated into four different types of financial statements which show different information about the corporation. These four major financial statements are the ones mentioned before—the Balance Sheet, the Income Statement, the Cash Flow Statement, and the Statement of Stockholder's Equity.

---

27. Dictionary of Finance and Investment Terms, published by Barron's, 9th edition, John Downes and Jordan Elliot Goodman.

You will be relieved to know that as an attorney, you will not actually draft the financial statements, so we will not review the creation of financial statements in detail. However, it is helpful to have a general idea of how financial statements are generated to be able to effectively read and review them. As lawyers, we do not record the financial transactions, determine how to record the transactions, or even advise whether the financial statements are accurate. Accountants will create the financial statements, help determine how to record the financial transactions, and finalize the financial statements. As an attorney, you are a user of these financial statements. You will use financial statements to identify potential legal issues for your clients as well as to help determine whether your clients are complying with, or violating, legal obligations your clients may have. You might, for example, use financial statements to help determine whether your client has been paying its debt obligations in accordance with a loan agreement or whether your client is at risk of assuming more debt than a current loan agreement allows. You can also use the financial statements to evaluate your client's liquidity or solvency and determine whether your client remains in compliance with a loan agreement that places restrictions on the corporation's financial condition, such as liquidity and solvency requirements.

Every financial transaction of the corporation must be recorded, and that recordation process begins at the time of the transaction. Let's revisit our fictional company, Widget Shoes, to explore this. When your friends decide to invest their hard-earned money to provide initial cash capital to Widget Shoes, that investment of cash in the corporation, which is completed by the sale of shares to your friends, is recorded. When this financial transaction occurs, the accountant, or your friends using accounting software, will create a Journal Entry which is a brief narrative describing the transaction. In other words, the corporation will need to track the cash the corporation received from selling shares and the number and types of shares the corporation sells. To accomplish this, the accountant will create an account and adjust the account balances with the results of each financial transaction—in this instance, the sale of shares in exchange for cash. So, if your friends pay cash to purchase $100,000 of shares on January 1, the accountant would write a narrative of the transaction as a Journal Entry and create an account called "Cash" with a new balance of $100,000 and an account called "Shares" with a new balance of $100,000. This shows that the corporation received $100,000 in cash and the corporation sold $100,000 of shares. By keeping a running tally of financial transactions and updating the account balances accordingly, the accountant can easily track the balance in each account. You may have heard the terms "debits" and "credits" in accounting. Those are accounting terms that reference whether the balance of an account is increasing or decreasing. However, those concepts are mostly applicable to how accountants create financial statements not how lawyers review financial statements. So, we will not make your eyes glaze over by covering them here. Here is a simplified version of how the Journal Entry transaction might be recorded for the Widget Shoes sale of shares for cash:

Widget Shoes Journal Entries

1/1/2019	Shares	$100,000 (+)
	Cash	$100,000 (+)

To record the issuance and sale of $100,000 shares for cash (the account balance for shares would increase to reflect the corporation's issuance of shares, and the account balance for cash would increase to reflect the corporation's receipt of cash).

Next, recall that the corporation rented some warehouse space. Let's assume that the lease was for $1,000 per month as of February 1. The accountant would create an account to record the expense of renting the warehouse and would also need to record paying out the $1,000 in cash in rent expense. So, that transaction might be recorded as follows:

Widget Shoes Journal Entries

1/1/2019	Shares	$100,000
	Cash	$100,000

To record the issuance and sale of $100,000 shares for cash.

2/1/2019	Rental Expense	$1,000 (+)
	Cash	$1,000 (-)

To record rental expense for renting warehouse (the account for rental expense would increase to reflect the increase in rental expense incurred, and the account for cash would decrease to reflect the corporation's expenditure of $1,000 in cash).

As you see, for every financial transaction, the accountant will record the transaction, creating new accounts as needed and updating existing accounts as needed.

However, for this information to be useful, the accountant will need to be able to easily see the balance in each account briefly. So, accountants will update the balance in each account every time a financial transaction increases or decreases that account's balance. After the above transaction, the account balances for the shares, cash and rental expense accounts would look as follows:

	Shares	Cash	Rental Expense
	$100,000	$100,000	$1,000
		–$1,000	
Balance	$100,000	$99,000	$1,000

At the end of the fiscal period, the accountant will take the balance from each account and display the name of the account and the balance of each account in a commonly used format on the financial statements. To see what a completed financial statement looks like, review the sample Balance Sheet in the next chapter.

Chapter 1 Highlights

- Learning the basics of business is helpful for law students, regardless of their practice area.
- Corporations are creations of state statute, so you must look to the state where the corporation is incorporated and operating to determine the applicable statutory law.
- Corporations are created by incorporators and governed by a Board of Directors who are elected by shareholders.

Two

Balance Sheet

- This chapter explains the Balance Sheet, the first of four major financial statements, and how it reflects a corporation's assets, liabilities and owner's equity.

- In this chapter, you will learn about liquidity and how that affects a corporation's ability to pay its debts as they become due.

- This chapter also briefly reviews a corporation's equity structure, including shares authorized, issued, and outstanding.

- You will learn that as an attorney, the Balance Sheet can help you determine whether your corporate client is complying with certain restrictions in loan agreements, the number of corporate shares issued and outstanding, whether the corporation's account balances are at the level required by investors and lenders, and help you identify potential financial trends that might have legal implications.

- This chapter includes a case study allowing you to analyze a Balance Sheet and how such analysis can be used in litigation in a small M&A deal.

A. Balance Sheet Overview

Fundamentally, the Balance Sheet tells you what the corporation owns, what the corporation owes, and how much profit has been invested into, and retained by, the corporation.

Quickly review the sample Balance Sheet below to familiarize yourself with how it is structured, the information that is available, and how the information is presented.

Sample Balance Sheet

Widget Shoes, Inc

Balance Sheet

ASSETS		Dec 31, 2020	Dec 31, 2019
Current assets:			
Cash	$	5,000	15,000
Marketable Securities		5,000	4,000
Accounts Receivable		10,000	6,000
Inventories		30,000	20,000
Other Current Assets		5,000	5,000
Total Current Assets:		55,000	50,000
Non-Current Assets:			
Loan to Owner	$	20,000	10,000
Property, Plant & Equipment		36,000	40,000
Less: Accumulated Depreciation		*4,000*	*4,000*
Net Property, Plant and Equipment		32,000	36,000
Goodwill		2,000	3,000
Other Intangible Assets		3,000	1,000
Total Intangible Assets		5,000	4,000
Total Non-Current Assets:		55,000	50,000
TOTAL ASSETS:	$	110,000	100,000

LIABILITIES	Dec 31, 2020	Dec 31, 2019
Current Liabilities:		
Accounts Payable	3,000	2,000
Salaries Payable	7,000	3,000
Notes Payable	5,000	5,000
Current Maturities of Long-Term Debt	3,000	3,000
Total Current Liabilities	18,000	13,000
Non-Current Liabilities:		
Long-Term Debt	42,000	45,000
Other Non-current liabilities	2,000	2,000
Total Non-Current Liabilities	44,000	47,000
TOTAL LIABILITIES:	62,000	60,000
SHAREHOLDER'S EQUITY ($1 Par Value; 1 mill shares authorized; 100,000 shares issued and outstanding)		
Common Stock	10,000	5,000
Add'tl Paid-in-Capital	40,000	40,000
Retained Earnings	(2,000)	(5,000)
Total Shareholder's Equity	48,000	40,000
TOTAL LIABILITIES AND SHAREHOLDER'S EQUITY:	110,000	100,000

B. Sections of the Balance Sheet

As you can see, the Balance Sheet is divided into three sections:

- **Assets** (Current Assets and Non-Current Assets)—the section on the top of the Balance Sheet, or simply what the corporation owns.

- **Liabilities** (Current Liabilities and Non-Current Liabilities)—the section in the middle of the Balance Sheet, or simply what the corporation owes.

- **Shareholder's Equity**—the section on the bottom of the Balance Sheet, or simply how much the owners have invested into the corporation and how much profit the corporation has retained in the corporation.

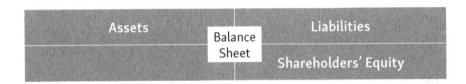

1. Assets

Assets are listed by the specific type of asset. A corporation will have different types of assets such as cash, inventory, and property, and each type of asset is listed on the Balance Sheet in a separate account. Assets are generally listed in two categories—current assets, meaning assets that are expected to be converted into cash within the next twelve months, and non-current assets, meaning assets that are not expected to be converted into cash within the next twelve months.

The current asset accounts on the Balance Sheet are listed in order of liquidity, meaning in the order of which assets can be converted to cash the quickest. Accordingly, cash—provided that the corporation has cash—will be the first account listed. The other major accounts, or types of current assets, that you will find in the current assets category in the assets section on a Balance Sheet are marketable securities (highly liquid investments that can easily be converted to cash), accounts receivables, inventory, and a catch-all of "other current assets"—worry not, these are explained further below. Non-current assets, also explained below, are either tangible assets, sometimes referred to as capital assets, or intangible assets such as intellectual property.

Now, one concept students frequently ask about is what does the value listed for an asset mean? Is that the fair market value of the asset or some other value? In this book, you will read about "book value" and "fair market value." These are another of those pesky accounting concepts. Unlike some other concepts that you do not need to understand in depth because … you know … you're not an accountant, book value and fair market value are accounting concepts that will impact your ability to review financial statements. Simply, book value refers to the value of an asset on the corporation's books. Fair market value simply refers to the value that a ready, willing, and able purchaser is willing to pay for that asset. Those values may be the same but often differ. These values often differ because of a concept called "depreciation" that we will cover in more detail when we discuss the Income Statement. For now, let us utilize our basic understanding that book value is the value of an asset as listed on the corporation's financial books, and that value can be, but is not always, different from the fair market value that a buyer is willing to pay for that asset.

a. Current Assets

Looking closer at the different line items, or accounts, in the Balance Sheet, let's start with current assets. Remember, accountants will determine how each financial transaction is recorded, and using that information, accountants will create the financial statements. So, we will focus on what you as an attorney will consider when reviewing final and published financial statements.

Cash is an easy concept to understand—it is the amount of cash the corporation has as of the date of the Balance Sheet. It is important for a corporation to track the amount of cash that it has on-hand, as cash is used to pay the costs of operating the corporation. To understand how this can help you as an attorney identify legal issues, think of our corporation, Widget Shoes. As you may recall from the corporation's previous Journal Entries, as of February 1, 2019, the corporation rented a warehouse and, thus, the corporation needed cash to pay the landlord the $1,000 monthly rent (you read these journal entries in the previous chapter, but they are restated here as a reference).

Widget Shoes Journal Entries

| 1/1/2019 | Shares | $100,000 |
| | Cash | $100,000 |

To record the issuance and sale of $100,000 of shares for cash (the shares account balance increases and the cash account balance increases).

| 2/1/2019 | Rental Expense | $1,000 |
| | Cash | $1,000 |

To record rental expense for renting a warehouse (the rental account balance increases and the cash account balance decreases).

Here are new transactions—On February 30, 2019, Widget Shoes hired workers to work in the warehouse to make the shoes and those employees will need to be paid. The accountants will record the cost of paying those employees in the corporation's financial records as shown below:

Widget Shoes Journal Entries

1/1/2019	Shares	$100,000
	Cash	$100,000

To record the issuance and sale of $100,000 shares for cash.

2/1/2019	Rental Expense	$1,000
	Cash	$1,000

To record rental expense for renting warehouse.

2/30/2019	Salary Expense	$500 (+)
	Cash	$500 (–)

To record salary expense for hiring workers (the account balance for salaries expense would increase to reflect the salary expense the corporation incurred, while the account balance for cash would decrease to reflect the expenditure of cash).

All these activities impact cash, so your clients will need to manage, and be able to carefully track, their cash balances. As an attorney, you will want to remain aware of whether your client's cash balance is sufficient to manage its legal obligations. For example, does your client have enough cash to pay its rent? If not, your client has legal exposure for a contract breach of its lease. Does your client have enough cash to pay its workers? As you can surmise, if, as in the above case, your client employs workers, the client will have the legal risk of violating federal and state wage laws if the employees are not paid for the work performed.

Additional major current asset accounts include:

Marketable Securities—Securities that are highly liquid, and thus, easily convertible to cash. These securities can include negotiable debt obligations of the US government, most notably Treasury Bills, often referred to as T-Bills.

Accounts Receivable—Accounts Receivable simply refer to the amount that a corporation is owed for inventory that the corporation has sold, but for which it has yet to receive payment, as part of the corporation's day-to-day business. For example, let us assume that Widget Shoes sold 3 pairs of shoes to a customer. That customer could either pay for those shoes in cash or pay for those shoes with a promise to pay. If the customer pays for the shoes in cash, that means that Widget's cash balance would increase because it received cash from the customer. If the customer pays for the shoes with a promise to pay, that means that Widget's accounts receivable balance would increase because it is now owed money.

Now, you might wonder why a customer's promise to pay Widget for shoes would be listed as an asset for Widget. Think of this question from the lawyer's standpoint: Widget and the customer entered into an agreement where Widget promised to sell, and the customer promised to buy, a pair of shoes for a specified amount of money. Here, Widget performed its obligations under the contract by conveying the shoes to the customer. Thus, now the customer is obligated to perform its obligations under the contract by paying Widget for the shoes. That, as you know from your rapt attention in your 1L Contracts class, is a legally binding contract. As you learned in Contracts, when a contract is breached, the non-breaching party has the right to recover monetary damages for that breach. In this case, Widget now has a legal right to the amount of money the customer originally promised to pay for those shoes. That legal right to receive money is an asset to Widget. If the customer does not pay, Widget has the legal right to sue to collect on the breached contract or Widget could sell its right to collect on the breached contract to a third party, such as a debt collector. In either case, Widget's right to collect is convertible to cash and, thus, is an asset to Widget.

Inventory—Inventory, broadly speaking, represents the book value of the items that a corporation intends to sell as part of that corporation's business operations. In the case of Widget, its inventory would be shoes.

Other Current Assets—These are other smaller assets that can be combined into a single account, such as office supplies, office furniture, and other smaller items.

b. Non-Current Assets

Non-current assets, again, are those assets that are not expected to be converted to cash within the next twelve months. Commonly, those assets are (i) loans to the owner, (ii) property, plant and equipment, (iii) long-term marketable securities, and (iv) intellectual property.

Loan to the Owner—This account is not always present, but it can present special challenges for you as an attorney. A loan to an owner, sometimes listed as "shareholder loan," occurs when the corporation lends money to one of the corporation's principals. In that case, the corporation's principal borrows money from the corporation with the stated intention of repaying the money to the corporation at some point in the future.

Legal Highlights

Loans to Owners

As the attorney to Widget, you would likely request that Widget's principal who is borrowing the money from Widget evidence this loan and the intent to repay the loan in a written loan agreement between Widget and the principal. As the attorney, you can identify potential legal issues:

- If this is a loan, is there interest charged?

---

continued

continued

> - If this is a loan, during the term of the loan, is the balance of the loan on Widget's Balance Sheet decreasing (meaning that the principal is repaying the loan and regularly decreasing the amount of money owed to Widget)?
>
> - Or, if this is a loan in name only and the principal is not repaying the loan, is Widget misrepresenting its financial position to investors and lenders who rely on Widget's financial statements to determine whether to invest or lend money? In other words, is listing this loan as an asset that is not truly convertible to cash because the loan is not being repaid, opening Widget to legal claims of financial fraud or misrepresentation?
>
> This is another example of the importance of an attorney understanding financial statements sufficiently enough to be able to identify potential legal risks to the client from a review of the financial statements.

Property, Plant, and Equipment—This account, commonly referred to as PP&E, generally reflects the corporation's property and plants, such as warehouses, office buildings, and factories. It also can include equipment such as machinery, equipment, furniture, fixtures, and some leasehold improvements.

Accumulated Depreciation—This account is a little trickier. When corporations purchase PP&E, the accountant will record that purchase as an asset. The general idea is that property, plant and equipment, as tangible assets, will devalue over time from use, wear, and tear. Thus, the account balance for PP&E should reflect that decrease in value and the resultant remaining useful life of that asset. For example, let us assume that on March 1, 2019, Widget bought $40,000 of equipment to produce shoes. As you know, the accountants would record this financial transaction in Widget's books as follows:

Widget Shoes Journal Entries

1/1/2019	Shares	$100,000
	Cash	$100,000
	To record the issuance and sale of $100,000 shares for cash.	
2/1/2019	Rental Expense	$1,000
	Cash	$1,000
	To record rental expense for renting warehouse.	
2/30/2019	Salary Expense	$500
	Cash	$500
	To record salary expense for hiring workers.	

| 3/01/2019 | Property, Plant and Equipment | $40,000 (+) |
| | Cash | $40,000 (−) |

To record the purchase of shoe-making equipment (the account balance for property, plant and equipment would increase to reflect the acquisition of the equipment, while the account balance for cash would decrease to reflect the expenditure of cash).

However, you can easily imagine that this equipment, like any other machinery (such as a smart phone), will deplete with use and the passage of time. The account value of that equipment needs to be decreased—in accounting parlance, it is *depreciated*—to reflect that depletion. Worry not, accountants will determine how to depreciate the PP&E and by how much; your role is to understand that such equipment will depreciate over time and that the accumulated amount of that depreciation is reflected on the Balance Sheet in an account called accumulated depreciation.

While the accountants manage the depreciation of PP&E, your role as the lawyer is to identify any potential legal issues that could arise from accumulated depreciation.

Intellectual Property—Copyrights, trademarks and patents are all assets as they have value and are owned by the corporation. Even though they are intangible assets, they are still assets and, thus, are listed on the Balance Sheet.

Goodwill—Goodwill is another slightly tricky concept. In essence, when one corporation acquires another corporation, the acquiring corporation must reflect

---

Legal Highlights

Accumulated Depreciation and Amortization

Financial statements are used by lenders, potential investors, and current investors to determine whether to provide a loan, whether to invest or whether to sell an existing ownership stake. As such, financial statements must be truthful, particularly if the company is a publicly traded company. Here, accumulated depreciation, and similarly, accumulated amortization discussed below, can be used to artificially inflate or deflate the company's assets which could be an intentional misrepresentation of the company's financial position and an intentional misrepresentation of the book value of a company's assets. Such a misrepresentation could be a violation of federal securities laws. Additionally, as you will see in the next chapter, amortization also reduces a company's taxable income and a company's net profit.

If a lender, particularly a federally chartered lender, unknowingly relies on the company's fraudulent misrepresentation of the company's net profit or if the company fraudulently misstates the company's taxable income to the Internal Revenue Service, your client could violate several federal and state laws.

that transaction, as with all financial transactions, on the acquiring corporation's financial statements. Conceptually, when a corporation acquires another corporation, the acquiring corporation would integrate the acquired corporation into the acquiring corporation's operations to create a seamless integration. However, there are some companies that have an intrinsic value that increases the acquired corporation's value to the acquiring corporation. When the fair market value of the consideration from the acquiring corporation exceeds the net value of the identifiable assets acquired and liabilities assumed of the acquired corporation, that difference must be recorded in the acquiring corporation's financial statements. Broadly speaking, that difference is reflected as *Goodwill*.

Goodwill often occurs when the acquired corporation has strong brand name value. This goodwill might be a result of the expected future economic benefits of the acquired corporation's reputation, strong customer loyalty, proprietary technology, or other intrinsic value that is not specifically reflected in the acquired corporation's recorded assets.

Consider the case study at the end of this chapter of Apple's acquisition of the music company Beats and the resulting goodwill to help you consider goodwill in a real transaction.

Accumulated Amortization—Accumulated Amortization is simply the intangible assets' version of accumulated depreciation. Like tangible assets, the book value of intangible assets is reduced over time and the accumulated amount of that reduction is called accumulated amortization. Simply put, accumulated amortization is the total amount of amortization, or depletion, of the intangible asset.

C. Chapter 2 Balance Sheet Exercises and Case Studies

Exercise 2.1—Accumulated Depreciation

What if your client decides to misrepresent the amount of accumulated depreciation to overstate its assets? In other words, your client's PP&E on its Balance Sheet should look like the left column below. But, instead, your client, to intentionally misrepresent its financial condition and make it appear as though its assets have a greater book value than they do, decreases its accumulated depreciation to make its PP&E on its Balance Sheet look like the right column:

ASSETS		Should be:	Misrepresentation:
Current assets:			
Cash	$	5,000	5,000
Marketable Securities		5,000	5,000

ASSETS		Should be:	Misrepresentation:
Accounts Receivable		10,000	10,000
Inventories		30,000	30,000
Other Current Assets		5,000	5,000
Total Current Assets:		55,000	55,000
Non-Current Assets:			
Loan to Owner	$	20,000	20,000
Property, Plant & Equipment		36,000	36,000
Less: Accumulated Depreciation		5,000	2,000
Net Property, Plant and Equipment		31,000	34,000
Intellectual Property		4,000	4,000
Less: Accumulated Amortization		*1,000*	*1,000*
Net Intellectual Property		3,000	3,000
Total Non-Current Assets:		54,000	57,000
TOTAL ASSETS:	$	109,000	112,000

As you can see, by changing the amount of the accumulated depreciation, the corporation's Balance Sheet will show that the corporation has higher total assets than with less accumulated depreciation. While GAAP allows accountants to choose a method for depreciating PP&E, if such adjustments are done fraudulently, what are some of the potential legal consequences?

Case Study 2.2—Apple's Acquisition of Beats and Resultant Goodwill

On May 28, 2014, Apple announced Apple's acquisition of the subscription streaming music service Beats Music and Beats Electronics, which made headphones, speakers and audio software.[1] In the announcement, Apple noted that it acquired the companies for approximately $3 billion which, according to the announcement, consisted of a purchase price of $2.6 billion and approximately $400 million that Apple said would vest over time.[2]

According to Apple's financial statements, this purchase resulted in goodwill. In the notes to its financial statements, Apple details the purchase and resultant goodwill as follows:

On July 31, 2014, the Company completed the acquisitions of Beats Music, LLC, which offers a subscription streaming music service, and Beats Electronics, LLC, which makes Beats® headphones, speakers and audio software (collectively, "Beats"). The total purchase price consideration for these acquisitions was $2.6 billion, which consisted

---

1. https://www.apple.com/newsroom/2014/05/28Apple-to-Acquire-Beats-Music-Beats-Electronics/.

2. *Id.*

primarily of cash, of which $2.2 billion was allocated to goodwill, $636 million to acquired intangible assets and $258 million to net liabilities assumed.... In conjunction with the Beats acquisitions, the Company issued approximately 5.1 million shares of its common stock to certain former equity holders of Beats. The restricted stock was valued at approximately $485 million based on the Company's common stock on the acquisition date. The majority of these shares, valued at approximately $417 million, will vest over time based on continued employment with Apple.[3]

Questions for Case Study 2.2

1. Now that you have seen an example of goodwill, can you identify some market factors that might prompt an acquiring corporation to purchase another corporation for an acquisition price that results in goodwill?

2. When a corporation purchases another corporation, part of the financial analysis both companies conduct is valuing the acquired corporation's assets and liabilities and projecting the future cash flow, if any, the acquired corporation could provide to the acquiring corporation. Would such potential future cash flow impact the purchase price an acquiring corporation would be willing to pay in the acquisition?

D. Sections of the Balance Sheet cont'd

1. Liabilities

Widget Shoes, Inc
Balance Sheet

ASSETS		Dec 31, 2020	Dec 31, 2019
Current assets:			
Cash	$	5,000	15,000
Marketable Securities		5,000	4,000
Accounts Receivable		10,000	6,000
Inventories		30,000	20,000
Other Current Assets		5,000	5,000
Total Current Assets:		55,000	50,000
Non-Current Assets:			
Loan to Owner	$	20,000	10,000
Property, Plant & Equipment		36,000	40,000

---

3. Apple 2015 Balance Sheet Note 4.

Less: Accumulated Depreciation		4,000	4,000
Net Property, Plant and Equipment		32,000	36,000
Intangible Assets		4,000	5,000
Less: Accumulated Amortization		1,000	1,000
Net Intangible Assets		3,000	4,000
Total Non-Current Assets:		55,000	50,000
TOTAL ASSETS:	$	110,000	100,000

LIABILITIES

Current Liabilities:

Accounts Payable	3,000	2,000
Salaries Payable	7,000	3,000
Notes Payable	5,000	5,000
Current Maturities of Long-Term Debt	3,000	3,000
Total Current Liabilities	18,000	13,000

Non-Current Liabilities:

Long-Term Debt	42,000	45,000
Other Non-current liabilities	2,000	2,000
Total Non-Current Liabilities	44,000	47,000
TOTAL LIABILITIES:	62,000	60,000

SHAREHOLDER'S EQUITY
($1 Par Value; 1 mill shares
authorized; 100,000 shares issued
and outstanding)

Common Stock	10,000	5,000
Add'tl Paid-in-Capital	40,000	40,000
Retained Earnings	(2,000)	(5,000)
Total Shareholder's Equity	48,000	40,000
TOTAL LIABILITIES AND SHAREHOLDER'S EQUITY:	110,000	100,000

Liabilities, located in the middle of the above Balance Sheet, reflect what a corporation owes. These obligations are a claim on the assets of the corporation and must be paid when due. Later, upon liquidation of the corporation, any unpaid liabilities are paid using the assets of the corporation. Liabilities are intuitively understandable by many law students because so many of you have law school loans—those are your liabilities. Your law school loans are obligations that you owe and must pay. Your law school loans, for example, represent a claim on your assets—subject to bankruptcy laws, your assets could be claimed to pay these liabilities, like how a corporation's liabilities represent a claim on the corporation's assets.

Like assets, liabilities are separated into current liabilities—those liabilities expected to be paid within the next twelve months—and non-current liabilities—those liabilities expected to be paid after the next twelve months.

As a user, if you want to know whether a corporation's assets (what it owns) exceed the corporation's liabilities (what it owes), you simply need to review the corporation's Balance Sheet to make that determination. Or, if you want to determine whether a corporation has very little liquid assets, you will simply look to the corporation's current assets on the Balance Sheet.

a. Current Liabilities

Like current assets, current liabilities are liabilities that are expected to be repaid within twelve months. Since current assets are expected to be converted to cash within twelve months and current liabilities are expected to be repaid within twelve months, current liabilities, like all liabilities, are claims on a corporation's assets and are expected to be repaid with current assets. So, when trying to determine a corporation's solvency, or its ability to pay its debts when they become due, you would compare a corporation's current assets to its current liabilities. If the current assets are greater than the corporation's current liabilities, barring some unforeseen circumstances, the corporation should be able to pay its current liabilities within the next fiscal year. This is not an absolute rule because an asset's book value is sometimes greater than its fair market value, especially if the corporation must sell its current assets quickly. There are many different types of current liabilities, but common current liability accounts are accounts payable, salaries payable, notes payable, and current maturities of long-term-debt, all discussed below.

Accounts Payable—Accounts Payable reflects the amount that the corporation owes to vendors, creditors and suppliers for goods, services and inventory purchased by the corporation.

Salaries Payable—Salaries Payable reflects the amount of salary that the corporation owes but has not yet paid. The balance in this account increases when the corporation employs workers and owes the workers' salaries and wages for services provided.

Notes Payable—Notes Payable represent the amount of short-term debt that the corporation owes. Since notes payable is a current liability, this is debt that is expected to become due by the end of the fiscal year.

Current Maturities of Long-Term Debt—Current Maturities of Long-Term Debt are simply the portion of a corporation's long-term debt that is expected to become due within the fiscal period. Think about it in the context of your student loans (yes, I hear the collective groans, but it's helpful context). When you graduate, you will have an exit interview where your school representatives will tell you the total amount you owe for your student loans, at which point I want you to *breathe*. Your student loan lender will also then remind you of the maximum number of years over which you are required to repay the loans. Assume that your loan repayment period is 10 years. In that case, your current maturities of long-term debt is the amount of your student loans that must be repaid in the current calendar year. Similarly for a corporation, the corporation's current maturities of long-term debt are the portion of the corporation's long-term debt that must be repaid within the fiscal period.

Legal Highlights
Insolvency

If the company's current liabilities are greater than the company's current assets, then the company might encounter cash flow issues or an inability to pay its current liabilities—meaning your client is "insolvent." As a lawyer, your client's inability to pay its legal obligations could subject the client to lawsuits for unpaid obligations such as unpaid salaries, shown as salaries payable, or short-term loans, shown as notes payable.

As you know, wages can become due pursuant to a verbal, written or implied contract and, hence, your client's inability to pay its current liabilities can reflect an inability to perform under its contracts. As you should recall from your first year Contracts class, non-performance of a contract is considered a breach and the breaching party is subject to remedies, including equitable or monetary remedies. If your review of the Balance Sheet indicates that your client is, or is becoming, insolvent, that review should prompt you to discuss the potential legal ramifications of this insolvency with your corporate client.

While how to address the insolvency is a business issue that your client will need to manage, insolvency presents many legal issues, such as those described here, that you can help your client resolve.

---

b. Non-Current Liabilities

Non-current liabilities are those liabilities that are expected to become due within the next twelve months. The most common non-current liability is long-term debt such as a mortgage or a long-term loan.

2. Shareholder's Equity

The last section on the Balance Sheet is shareholder's equity. Mathematically, the shareholder's equity is the corporation's assets minus its liabilities. In other words, after the assets are used to pay the corporation's liabilities, what is left is considered shareholder's equity. Conceptually, the section on shareholder's equity presents information about the shareholders' investment into the corporation, the corporation's profits retained, and the losses incurred by the corporation over time.

a. Common Stock and Preferred Stock

If you look at the shareholder's equity section on the above Balance Sheet, you will first see information on common stock, par value, additional paid-in-capital, and references to authorized shares, issued shares and outstanding shares. When an investor in a corporation purchases ownership in the corporation, the corporation issues stock to the investor. That stock is a unit of ownership in that corporation. The owners of stock are called shareholders. Generally, corporations will issue some variation of two types of stock: common stock and preferred stock. Common stock is the most frequent stock issued. Common stock shareholders, by the law of the state corporations statute, are the shareholders who elect the Board of Directors. Preferred stock is stock that, depending on the rights set forth in the state corporations statute, can provide preferences for the payment of dividends and in the liquidation of the corporation. Preferred stock shareholders can also have special voting rights. Depending on the state, preferred stock obtains these rights by statute, by inclusion in the Articles of Incorporation, by resolution of the Board of Directors, or by contract between the corporation issuing the preferred stock and the investor investing money in the corporation.

Regardless, common stock and preferred stock both represent ownership in the corporation and, thus, like any other financial transaction, when the common or preferred stock are issued from the corporation to the shareholder, that issuance and transfer of ownership must be recorded in the books of the corporation. So, when common stock and preferred stock are issued, the compensation received for that stock issuance must be recorded as well. The book value, or par value, of the stock must be recorded in addition to any excess above par value, known as additional paid-in-capital. Thus, when viewing the shareholder's equity portion of the Balance Sheet, you will commonly see the par value of the common stock and preferred stock issued as well as any amount above the par value that the corporation received as consideration for issuing the stock to the investor.[4] We will discuss preferred stock and common stock and their differences in more detail later in the book in the chapter on Equity Analysis.

b. Retained Earnings

You will also see retained earnings on the Balance Sheet. At the end of the corporation's fiscal year, the corporation, if it has had a profitable year, will have a profit. The corporation must decide what to do with that profit. Many shareholders want the corporation to return that profit to shareholders; after all, earning a profit and

---

4. Not all states require shares to have par value. For example, Illinois requires shares to have a par value while Delaware does not.

receiving that profit in cash from the corporation is one of the main reasons many entrepreneurs create, or investors invest in, a corporation.[5] Corporations often will face shareholder revolt if corporations do not return at least some of the profit to the owners of the corporation, the shareholders. However, corporations cannot function for long without sufficient capital to sustain the corporation. The corporation's Board of Directors must balance distributing a portion of the profit to the shareholders and retaining some of the profit in the corporation to enable the corporation to remain sustainable. That portion of the corporation's profits that is distributed to shareholders is distributed by issuing dividends to the shareholders. Broadly, that portion of the corporation's profit that the Board of Directors decides to retain in the corporation is shown as retained earnings.

Overall, the shareholder's equity section of the Balance Sheet simply shows how much shareholders have invested in the corporation and how much of the corporation's profit the Board of Directors has determined to retain in the corporation's coffers.

c. Authorized, Issued, Outstanding Shares and Treasury Stock

As you may recall from previous readings, corporations are formed pursuant to state corporations statutes. Many of these statutes require corporations to determine, upon formation, the number of shares that the corporation will be allowed to sell, or in finance parlance—*to issue*. At some point, these shares are sold to shareholders and, on occasion, the corporation who issued the shares might repurchase those shares back from shareholders.

While there is an entire body of law governing these issues which we will not cover here, overall:

- *Authorized Shares* reflects the number of shares that the corporation will be allowed to issue to shareholders.

- *Issued Shares* reflects the number of authorized shares that the corporation has sold to shareholders.

- *Treasury Stock* reflects the value of issued shares that the corporation has repurchased.

- *Outstanding Shares* reflects the number of issued shares that the corporation has not yet repurchased.

---

5. Delaware Code § 170 Dividends; payment; wasting asset corporations.
    (a) The directors of every corporation, subject to any restrictions contained in its certificate of incorporation, may declare and pay dividends upon the shares of its capital stock either:
        (1) Out of its surplus, as defined in and computed in accordance with §§ 154 and 244 of this title; or
        (2) In case there shall be no such surplus, out of its net profits for the fiscal year in which the dividend is declared and/or the preceding fiscal year.

E. Review of Major Accounts on the Balance Sheet

For your reference, these are some of the major accounts that you will find on the Balance Sheet, most of which have already been discussed. This is not an exhaustive list, and companies will often adjust the name of an account for their own purposes. However, for your reference, these are some of the more common ones.

Assets
Accounts Receivable
Accumulated Amortization
Accumulated Depreciation
Cash and Cash Equivalents
Goodwill
Investments
Inventory
Patents, Trademarks, and Copyrights
Prepaid Expenses
Property, Plant and Equipment
  (PP&E)
Supplies

Liabilities and Equity
Liabilities
Accounts Payable
Current Maturities of
  Long-Term Debt
Interest Payable
Loans Payable
Long Term Debt
Notes Payable
Rent Payable
Salaries Payable
Taxes Payable
Unearned Revenue

Equity
Additional Paid-in-Capital
Common Stock
Dividends
Owner Contributions
Preferred Stock
Retained Earnings
Treasury Stock

Whew! You made it through your second chapter on Business Fundamentals! For some of you, you will find this fascinating and wonder why you avoided business for so long. For many others, this will feel like learning a new language, as the quantitative analysis is different than the qualitative analysis to which you may have been accustomed. It's ok—the concepts may be new, but with a little patience, time and probably some frustration, you will hear some business news on the TV or hear some business concepts at work and realize that the language is no longer foreign to you and you will realize this was worth it.

F. Chapter 2 Balance Sheet Exercises and Case Studies cont'd

Using the same sample Balance Sheet from earlier in the chapter, reproduced below, answer the following problems:

Widget Shoes, Inc.
Balance Sheet

ASSETS		Dec 31, 2020	Dec 31, 2019
Current assets:			
Cash	$	5,000	15,000
Marketable Securities		5,000	4,000
Accounts Receivable		10,000	6,000
Inventories		30,000	20,000
Other Current Assets		5,000	5,000
Total Current Assets:		55,000	50,000
Non-Current Assets:			
Loan to Owner	$	20,000	10,000
Property, Plant & Equipment		36,000	40,000
Less: Accumulated Depreciation		4,000	4,000
Net Property, Plant and Equipment		32,000	36,000
Intangible Assets		4,000	5,000
Less: Accumulated Amortization		1,000	1,000
Net Intangible Assets		3,000	4,000
Total Non-Current Assets:		55,000	50,000
TOTAL ASSETS:	$	110,000	100,000
LIABILITIES			
Current Liabilities:			
Accounts Payable		3,000	2,000
Salaries Payable		7,000	3,000
Notes Payable		5,000	5,000
Current Maturities of Long-Term Debt		3,000	3,000
Total Current Liabilities		18,000	13,000
Non-Current Liabilities:			
Long-Term Debt		42,000	45,000

Other Non-current liabilities	2,000	2,000
Total Non-Current Liabilities	44,000	47,000
TOTAL LIABILITIES:	62,000	60,000

SHAREHOLDER'S EQUITY
($1 Par Value; 1 mill shares
authorized; 100,000 shares issued
and outstanding)

Common Stock	10,000	5,000
Add'tl Paid-in-Capital	40,000	40,000
Retained Earnings	(2,000)	(5,000)
Total Shareholder's Equity	48,000	40,000
TOTAL LIABILITIES AND SHAREHOLDER'S EQUITY:	110,000	100,000

Exercise 2.3—Balance Sheet Analysis

These questions are designed to be simple. The goal here is to help familiarize you with identifying information on financial statements so when your client discusses their year-end cash balance, you will intuitively know on which financial statement, and where on that financial statement, that information is located. Students new to business can sometimes find financial statements intimidating. You will find that financial statements are not nearly as imposing once you start digging into them a bit. So, let's start with some easy questions.

1. Your client, Widget Shoes, asks you to review its compliance with some covenants in its loan agreement. To determine the company's compliance, you must first obtain financial information about Widget's financial condition by answering the following:

    a. How much cash did Widget have as of the end of FYE 2020?[6]

    b. By how much did Widget's accounts receivables change from FYE 2019 to FYE 2020?

    c. Are Widget's total current assets greater than Widget's total current liabilities as of FYE 2020? If so, by how much?

    d. What is the total of Widget's cash and marketable securities as of FYE 2019 and FYE 2020?

    e. What is the difference in Widget's total assets and its total liabilities for FYE 2020?

---

6. FYE is an abbreviation for Fiscal Year End.

2. If your client, a major bank, asked you to determine whether the borrower, Widget Shoes, breached a covenant in their loan agreement stating that the borrower's 2020 fiscal year-end cash cannot be less than $10,000, what would your answer be?

3. If your client, a potential investor, asks you whether Widget has sold any common stock to investors yet, where would you look and what is your answer?

4. It is January 1, 2021. You work for a law firm hired to write a document outlining Widget's issuance of stock. As part of the drafting, your law partner asks you whether Widget sold any common stock the previous year. Where would you look to find the answer and what would your answer be?

5. You work for a bank that has lent money to Widget Shoes. What are some of the legal questions raised by your review of the Balance Sheet? Remember that just because there is a legal question, does not mean that there is a legal issue. It simply means that you can identify potential legal issues from a review of the Balance Sheet.

6. How many shares is Widget authorized to issue to investors?

7. Widget's common stock account shows a 2020 year-end balance of $10,000. Did Widget receive a cash total of $10,000 for the issuance of the common stock in 2020?

Case Study 2.4 — Marlie Farms

Marlie Farms ("Business") is being sold to Browton, Inc. ("Buyer"). You represent the owners of Business ("Seller") in this transaction. Your role is to negotiate the Asset Purchase Agreement ("Agreement") and help client in any resultant disputes regarding the Agreement. The parties negotiate for Buyer to purchase Business for over $527,800. Opposing counsel representing Buyer agrees to draft the Agreement which is the agreement by which Buyer will purchase the specified assets of Business. After the conclusion of the purchase, your client, Seller, receives notice that Buyer is suing Seller for breach of contract. You review the complaint and note that Buyer's complaint argues that Seller did not convey all of the assets that Buyer argues should have been conveyed pursuant to the Agreement. Perplexed, you review the Agreement and note the following provisions and exhibits:

Recitals

Buyer will purchase substantially all of the machinery, equipment, inventory, goodwill, assets, real estate, paraphernalia and trade name of the Business, Business Real Estate and Residence.

Section 3—Obligations of the Parties

3A—Purchase of Assets

Seller agrees to sell, and Buyer agrees to purchase, the following assets of Business:

a. Business Real Estate;

b. Residence;

c. Accounts Receivable of Marlie Farms;

d. Cash on hand/bank account(s), and any prepaid insurance, along with the right to any refunds or credits from any such prepaid insurance of Business;

e. Finished inventory of Business;

f. Raw material inventory of Business;

g. The machinery, equipment, including any and all vehicles owned by Business, fixtures, tools and furniture located at the locations of the Business in Ridgeland, SC and Allendale, SC.

h. Business' rights to use the trade name Marlie Farms, all customer lists, trade secrets, goodwill, technical product information, system documentation and other general administrative information required to operate and support the business.

Exhibit 3—Balance Sheet of Business

Marlie Farms, Inc.	Balance Sheet as of May 8, 2008 ASSETS		
Current Assets			
Cash			
	Cash/Checking	$14,285	
	Profit Sharing-Savings	$450	
	Total Cash		$14,735
Accounts Receivable			
	Accounts Receivable	$170,019	
	Total Accounts Receivable		$170,019
Inventory			
	Finished Inventory		
	FP-Hangers	$139,412	

FP-Barrels	$320	
FP-Corn	$77,846	
FP-Gazing Globes	$416,191	
Total Finished Inventory	$633,769	
Materials Inventory		
RM Inventory-Globes	$814	
RM Inventory-Steel	$23,933	
RM Inventory-Packaging	$43,132	
RM Inventory-Point of Sales	$109,536	
RM Inventory-Paint & chemicals	$37,864	
RM Inventory-Ornaments	$2,977	
RM Inventory-Other	$14,387	
Not Stock Inventory	$515,507	
Total Materials Inventory	$748,149	
Work in Process		
WIP-Materials	$15,671	
Total Work in Process	$15,671	
Total Inventory		$1,397,589

Other Current Assets

Loans to Shareholders	$327,123	
Insurance Premiums	$13,339	
Total Other Current Assets		$340,462

Total Current Assets $1,922,806

Non-Current Assets

Fixed Assets

Property & Equipment Tools	$72,695	
Leasehold Improvements	$211,385	

Machinery & Equipment	$307,242	
Vehicles	$20,000	
Total Property & Equipment	$611,322	
Accumulated Depreciation		
Acmltd Dpr-Leasehold Improve	$(69,797)	
Acmltd Dpr-Machinery & Equipment	$(370,415)	
Acmltd Dpr-Vehicles	$(18,010)	
Loan Closing Costs	$3,486	
Accumulated Amortization	$6,414	
Total Accumulated Depreciation	$(448,321)	
Total Fixed Assets		$163,002

Other Assets

Other Assets		
Utility Deposit	$412	
Total Other Assets	$412	
Total Other Assets		$412
Total Assets		$2,086,220

LIABILITIES AND EQUITY

Current Liabilities
Accounts Payable

Accounts Payable	$221,118	
Total Accounts Payable		$221,118

Other Payables

	Accrue Purchase Orders	$799	
	Notes Payable-L Robinson	$271,388	
	Notes Payable-L Robinson	$85,000	
	R & F Imports	$129,981	
	Line of Credit-Main Bank	$1,043,276	
	Main Bank-from LOC	$69,154	
	Total Other Payables		$1,599,597

Payroll Taxes Payable

	Federal Payroll Taxes Payable	$1,115	
	State Payroll Taxes Payable	$547	
	Federal UC Taxes Payable (ERFUTA)	$10	
	State UC Taxes Payable (ERSUTA)	$(1,802)	
	Total Payroll Taxes Payable		$(130)

Taxes Payable

	Sales Tax/Use Tax	$(15)	
	Total Taxes Payable		$(15)
	Total Current Liabilities		$1,820,570

Non-Current Liabilities
Long-Term Liabilities

	Bank Debt		
	Notes: Jay & Kay, LLC	$553,917	
	NOTES: Bill Booker	$49,142	
	NOTES: Sister Love	$40,898	
	Total Bank Debt	$643,957	

Total Long-Term Liabilities		$643,957
Total Liabilities		$2,464,526
Shareholders' Equity		
Common Stockholders		
Common Stock	$1,000	
Treasury Stock-Principal	$(192,944)	
Treasury Stock-Interest	$(7,574)	
Retained Earnings	$(340,758)	
Total Common Stockholders		$(540,276)
Total Net Income		$161,972
Total Shareholders' Equity		$(378,304)
Total Liabilities and Equity		$2,086,223

To understand the Buyer's legal argument, you first look to answer the following questions about Business' FYE (Fiscal Year End) accounts. Again, these questions are designed to be easy to familiarize you with the Balance Sheet:

Questions for Case Study 2.4—Marlie Farms

1. What is the FYE balance of Business' accounts receivable?

2. What is the Business' FYE balance of cash?

3. What is the Business' FYE balance of Prepaid Insurance (listed above as Insurance Premiums)?

4. What is the Business' FYE balance of Finished Inventory?

5. What is the Business' FYE balance of Raw Materials Inventory (Materials Inventory)?

6. What is the Business' FYE balance of Machinery and Equipment (excluding accumulated depreciation)?

7. What is the Business' FYE balance of Vehicles owned by Seller (excluding accumulated depreciation)?

8. What is the Business' FYE balance of Tools?

You set up a conference call with Buyer, and Buyer relays their assessment of the history:

Business had loans with Main Bank ("Bank") for about $2 million, and Business' owners personally guaranteed those loans. Business was struggling, and Bank wanted out of its loan. Soon thereafter, Sellers approached Buyer about Buyer purchasing Business' assets and real estate for almost $530,000. Buyer reviewed Business' Balance Sheet showing Business had total assets of about $2 million. Sellers then took Buyer on a tour of Business' facilities, during which, according to Buyer's attorney, Sellers told Buyer that everything in the buildings and grounds goes with the sale.

At a subsequent meeting with Bank, Bank agreed that if Buyer were to purchase Business' assets for $535,000, and remit that sum to Bank to pay down the loan, Bank would write off the remaining indebtedness and discharge Sellers from their personal guaranties.

According to Buyer's attorney, the biggest issue concerned the shareholder loans. According to Buyer's attorney, Sellers owed Business $327,123.20 from a shareholder loan. This loan was a corporate asset shown on Business' Balance Sheet. According to Buyer's attorney, this was a loan from Business to Sellers resulting from Sellers taking distributions from Business in excess of Business' profits. Buyer's attorney argues that because it is a loan, Sellers are obligated to pay the loan back.

Buyer's attorney argues that by the terms of the Agreement, all assets of Business were being sold in the transaction and this shareholder loan should have been included.

Review the provisions above and review the Balance Sheet. What arguments do you make in the negotiations and to the court rebutting Buyer's position that the shareholder loans were to be conveyed pursuant to the Agreement?

This case study and the financial statements are from a case in Indiana. Now that you have reviewed the issues, review the court's findings in the excerpt from the court opinion that follows.

Whiskey Barrel Planters Co. v. American Gardenworks, Inc.

966 N.E.2d 711
Court of Appeals of Indiana
April 16, 2012, Decided; April 16, 2012, Filed

American GardenWorks is an Indiana corporation and MRE is an Indiana unlimited liability company, each with its principal place of business in Attica, Indiana. Both entities are wholly owned by Millennium Supply Company, which is owned by Gene McGowen ("McGowen") and Charles Neff.

Whiskey Barrel Planters was a family-owned Indiana business corporation and RFE is a limited liability corporation, each with its principal place of business in Boswell, Indiana. Ralph and Ann are the sole shareholders of Whiskey Barrel Planters and the sole members of RFE.

Whiskey Barrel had loans from Key Bank in the amount of approximately $2 million. The loans were secured by mortgages on Whiskey Barrel's business real estate and Ralph and Ann's residential property. Ralph and Ann had personally guaranteed the loans, and by the Spring of 2008, the bank began putting pressure on Ralph and Ann to secure other financing.

Because he was unable to secure additional financing, Ralph began looking for a buyer, and McGowen and Neff, acting as AGW's agents, agreed to buy Whiskey Barrel for $527,800. Although the bank was involved in the sale by putting time limitations thereon, the parties dealt at arm's length as sophisticated entities that had been in business for years. Indeed, prior to the sale, McGowen did a walkthrough inspection, and there is no evidence that he didn't see all of the property during the walkthrough. Both parties had the benefit of attorneys and accountants, and AGW's attorney drafted the "Asset Purchase Agreement" (the "Agreement"). In essence, both parties leapt at the perceived benefits of the sale, with the Robinsons looking at getting rid of debt and AGW acquiring assets at a discounted price. The bank approved the agreement and agreed to discharge Ralph's and Ann's personal guarantees and forgive any deficiency on the loan upon payment of the purchase amount to the bank.

The Agreement detailing the terms of AGW's acquisition of the specific assets of Whiskey Barrel was drafted and executed on June 30, 2008 by AGW's attorney, and it provided that "AGW assume[s] no debts, liabilities, or obligations incurred by [Whiskey Barrel] ... [and Whiskey Barrel] shall indemnify and hold [AGW] harmless thereon." (App. 420). Furthermore, Recital E of the Agreement provided that "[Whiskey Barrel] desire[s] to sell and AGW desire[s] to buy substantially all of the machinery, equipment, inventory, goodwill, assets, real estate, paraphernalia and trade name of the Business, Business Real Estate, and Residence."

Section 1, entitled "Purchase of Assets," defined the types of assets purchased, and provided:

[Whiskey Barrel] agrees to sell, and AGW agree[s] to purchase, the following assets of [Whiskey Barrel] .... :

    a. Business Real Estate, whose legal description is set forth in attached Exhibit A;

    b. Residence, whose legal description is set forth in attached Exhibit B;

    c. Accounts Receivable of Whiskey Barrel;

    d. Cash on hand/bank account(s), and any prepaid insurance, along with the right to any refunds or credits from any such prepaid insurance of Whiskey Barrel;

e. Finished inventory of Whiskey Barrel;

f. Raw materials inventory of Whiskey Barrel;

g. The machinery, equipment, including any and all vehicles owned by Whiskey Barrel, fixtures, tools and furniture located at the locations of the Business in Boswell, Indiana and Foresman, Indiana, as set forth on the attached Exhibit C.

h. Whiskey Barrel's rights to use the trade name Whiskey Barrel Planters, all customer lists, trade secrets, goodwill, technical product information, system documentation and other general administrative information required to operate and support the Business.

On November 12, 2008, AGW filed a complaint against Whiskey Barrel, alleging eight counts. The complaint was amended on January 9, 2009, with the same counts. On April 29, 2009, AGW filed a second amended complaint, alleging thirteen counts. At issue in this appeal is Count III, wherein AGW alleges that it was entitled to collect as assets the loans by Whiskey Barrel to Ralph and Ann in the amount of $327,123.00 that were not included as accounts receivable but were shown on the *balance sheets* and tax returns of Whiskey Barrel as "Other Current Assets." (App. 184). Also at issue is Count VII, wherein AGW alleges that it was entitled to collect as assets 2008 Purdue football season tickets that were purchased by Ralph with Whiskey Barrel funds.

On June 10, 2009, Whiskey Barrel filed a motion for partial summary judgment as to, among other things, Counts III and VII…. The accompanying brief stated that shareholder loans "were not included as an asset by Whiskey Barrel to [AGW], as demonstrated by the [Agreement] and the *balance sheet* [AGW] attached to their Second Amended Complaint." (App. 224–25). The brief further stated that the evidence proffered by AGW—the *balance sheet* of Whiskey Barrel attached to [AGW's] second amended complaint—"refutes any notion that a 'loan to a shareholder' is included as part of the 'Accounts Receivable of Whiskey Barrel' which [AGW] acquired from [Whiskey Barrel]." (App. 225). The brief set forth further arguments that will be addressed below.

The motion for partial summary judgment also alleged that the second amended complaint failed as a matter of law because Section 1 of the Agreement did not provide for the sale of the 2008 Purdue football season tickets. The accompanying brief pointed out that the tickets were not denominated as "assets" sold pursuant to the Agreement.

AGW responded to Whiskey Barrel's motion for partial summary judgment and stated that the term "Accounts Receivable," as used in the Agreement, was ambiguous, and the term's meaning could not be determined as a matter of law. Thus, AGW alleged that the court could look outside the four corners of the Agreement to ascertain whether shareholder loans could be included as one of the "Accounts Receivable" that it purchased. AGW also responded that it was impossible to conclude, as a matter of law, that the 2008 Purdue football season tickets were not assets sold by Whiskey Barrel to AGW under the Agreement. In support of its response on both counts, AGW designated McGowen's affidavit, in which he opined:

It was the intention of both parties in executing the [Agreement] and completing the transaction that [AGW, as purchaser, was] buying all of the assets owned by [Whiskey Barrel], as [seller]. This included the *shareholder loan*, listed on the May 2008 *balance sheet* of [Whiskey Barrel], attached to [AGW's] Second Amended Complaint as Exhibit 3, and the season tickets for Purdue football, which are owned by and were ordered by Whiskey Barrel and were sent to Whiskey Barrel's Boswell address. After examining the books of [Whiskey Barrel], I confirmed that Whiskey Barrel had purchased the football tickets, and therefore such tickets were an asset of the company as of June 30, 2008.

As described above, the Agreement provided for the purchase of "*substantially all* of the machinery, equipment, inventory, goodwill, assets, real estate, paraphernalia and trade name of the Business, Business Real Estate, and Residence." (App. 418) (Emphasis added). The Agreement then listed the eight specific types of assets that were to be sold, a list including "Accounts Receivable of Whiskey Barrel" but not shareholder loans. (App. 418–19). Citing Webster's New College Dictionary, p. 1126 (4th ed. 2008), AGW notes that the term "substantial" is defined as "relating to or having substance." *Id.* AGW's Br. at 11. Thus, AGW reasons that the Agreement provides for the sale of "all assets of any substance." *Id.* AGW identifies the shareholder loans as such assets.

The adjective "substantial," however, is not used in the Agreement. Instead, the Agreement notes AGW's intent to buy "substantially all" of the assets. In this context, the word "substantially" is an adverb which is used to modify the adjective "all." The statement making the reference to AGW's purchase of "substantially all" of the assets explains the parties' intent regarding the type and quantity of assets to be sold. The plain and ordinary meaning of the term "substantially all" indicates "most but not all of the assets." As the drafter of the Agreement, AGW could have shown the sale of all assets by stating the sale was for "all of Whiskey Barrel's assets" or "all Whiskey Barrel assets including but not limited to the following." There is no ambiguity in this portion of the Agreement, and there is no reason to look outside the contract to extrinsic evidence.[2]

In its response to Whiskey Barrel's motion for partial summary judgment, AGW contended that the term "Accounts Receivable of Whiskey Barrel" was not defined in the four corners of the Agreement and was therefore ambiguous. AGW also contended that the term "accounts receivable" may refer to more than accounts to be paid by customers....

---

2. Accordingly, there is no basis for an exception to the parol evidence rule, and the evidence designated by AGW should not have been considered by the trial court.

The **_balance sheet_** attached to the second amended complaint by AGW and designated as evidence by Whiskey Barrel is unequivocal evidence of the meaning of "Accounts Receivable of Whiskey Barrel" as that term is used by AGW in the Agreement that it drafted. The **_balance sheet_** clearly shows that the term "accounts receivable," as used in the Agreement, does not include the shareholder loans (designated as "Other Current Assets,["] not "Accounts Receivable"). (App. 184). McGowen's unsupported claim does not rise to the level of evidence that creates a genuine issue of material fact on this issue. Accordingly, the trial court erred in denying Whiskey Barrel's motion for partial summary judgment on this issue.

Exercise 2.5 — Whiskey Planters

1. Now that you have read the case, discuss in class or with your classmates, what, if anything, could either lawyer have done differently for their client to avoid this dispute?

2. Do you think what you are learning now would be helpful were you to litigate a case such as this? If so, how?

Chapter 2 Highlights

- The Balance Sheet is one of four major financial statements.
- The Balance Sheet tells you what a corporation owns and what it owes.
- Current Assets are generally assets that the corporation expects to convert to cash within the next twelve months.
- Current Liabilities are generally liabilities that the corporation expects to pay within the next twelve months.
- The Balance Sheet shows an account balance as of the date the Balance Sheet is created.

Three

Income Statement

- This chapter explains the Income Statement, the second of the four major financial statements, and how it reflects a corporation's revenue and expenses and thus shows the income that a corporation earned, as well as the expenses incurred, over the fiscal period.

- Among other issues, this chapter details how the Income Statement enables lawyers to evaluate metrics such as whether a client is generating sufficient revenue to meet sales targets required in business contracts, whether a client is expending more expenses as a percentage of revenue than a loan agreement permits, and whether a client is generating enough net profit to return dividends to shareholders.

- This chapter also provides a case study examining the impact of a corporation's decision to expense an item or to convert it to a capitalized cost so that law students can understand how a corporation can manage its net income or loss, and thus attempt to manage its stock performance, through these accounting measures.

A. Income Statement Overview

The Income Statement tells you the amount of revenue that a corporation has generated over the course of the fiscal period, the amount of expenses the corporation has incurred over the course of the fiscal period, and the amount of profit that the corporation has generated over the course of the fiscal period.

As you should recall from the chapter on Balance Sheets, your client, Widget Shoes has begun operations and is now selling its shoes. However, your client realizes that it needs additional capital to continue operations and wants to meet with a friend who might be willing to lend Widget money for its operations. The potential lender asks Widget whether Widget is generating a profit. How does Widget know? Profit arises when a corporation generates revenue, pays its expenses and then has money left over. Sounds reasonable, yes? But how would Widget know how much revenue it has generated, how much it has paid in expenses and how much, if anything, is remaining? This is the basic purpose of the Income Statement—to display to the user the calculation of a corporation's net profit. When you review an Income Statement, you will see that the Income Statement begins with:

1. **Revenue:** how much revenue a corporation has generated,
2. **Cost of Goods Sold:** then shows how much the corporation has expended acquiring and producing the corporation's inventory for sale in its operations,
3. **Operating Expenses:** then shows how much the corporation has expended operating the corporation (paying wages to employees, paying rent, paying utilities, etc),
4. **Tax and Interest Expenses:** then shows how much the corporation has expended in taxes and interest for the fiscal period,
5. **Amortization and Depreciation Expenses:** then shows how much the corporation has allocated to amortization and depreciation for the fiscal period,
6. **Net Profit:** and ends with the corporation's net profit—what remains of the corporation's revenue after paying for all of the above costs to operate the corporation over the fiscal period.

Not to terrify those math-phobes amongst you who just *knew* you were done with math when you escaped—I mean finished—Algebra in high school, but the Income Statement is ultimately one long math equation that fundamentally looks like this:

Revenue (Item 1 above) − Costs & Expenses (Items 2–5 above) = Net Profit (Item 6 above)

Everything on the Income Statement simply explains how the final net profit resulted from the corporation's overall revenue. Take a look at the following sample Income Statement to get familiar with its layout, noting again, that it really is just one long equation:

Sample Income Statement

For the period ending December 31, 2018 (in dollars)

Revenue	$10,000,000
Less: Cost of Goods Sold	$2,000,000
= Gross Profit	$8,000,000
Operating Expenses	
Less: Selling, general and administrative expenses	$1,000,000
Less: Utility expenses	$500,000
Less: Rental expenses	$500,000
Less: Salary expenses	$500,000
Less: Depreciation expenses	$500,000
Less: Amortization expenses	$250,000
= Operating Income	$4,750,000
Less: Interest Expense	$250,000
Less: Tax Expense	$500,000
= Net Profit	$4,000,000

As you can see, the Income Statement begins with how much revenue the corporation earned over the fiscal period, then deducts from the revenue the expenses the corporation has incurred over the fiscal period, then concludes by calculating how much net profit the corporation has left after deducting those expenses. Note this terminology—(i) revenue and income are *earned* and (ii) expenses are *incurred*. While this language is not always used with such precision in industry, you can confidently refer to revenue and income as *earned* and expenses as *incurred* and you will be using correct lingo.

The Income Statement is quite logical and often the most intuitive of the four major financial statements. It will be very useful for you in practice.

> ### Legal Highlights
>
> *Income Statement*
>
> If your client has a requirement to generate a minimum amount of revenue to satisfy the corporation's investors, you can easily look at the top line of the Income Statement to determine if the requirement is satisfied.
>
> If your client has a requirement in a loan agreement to keep its rental expense below a certain amount, you can easily look on the Income Statement to determine your client's compliance with its loan requirements.

Let us take a moment now to walk together through the different sections and accounts on the Income Statement.

While the Balance Sheet tells you a corporation's financial condition as of a specific point in time, the Income Statement displays the accumulated values of each account over the fiscal period. In other words, when you see the revenue amount on the Income Statement, that simply means the amount of revenue that the corporation has earned over the fiscal period. For example, if I were to ask you to look at the Income Statement on the previous page and tell me how much revenue the corporation earned during the fiscal period, you would say $10,000,000. If I were to ask you how much that corporation incurred in rental expense for the fiscal period, you would say $500,000. If your law firm partner asked you what the corporation's net profit for the fiscal year end was, you would look at the Income Statement and first (i) verify that the Income Statement was for the fiscal year and not the month or quarter, and then (ii) respond with confidence that the corporation netted $4,000,000 that year.

Now that you have an overview of the Income Statement, its purpose and layout, we will now walk through the major accounts you are likely to find on most Income Statements you will encounter. Please note that different companies can use different accounts on their financial statements to personalize their financial statements to their corporate needs; however, most financial statements will have many if not most of the major accounts described below, so familiarizing yourself with the major accounts will give you a solid foundation for practice.

1. Revenue, Cost of Goods Sold, and Gross Profit

Revenue—Broadly, revenue is the amount of income that the corporation has earned during the fiscal period. Generally, a corporation earns revenue from the sale of inventory or services. To help understand this, visualize the transaction of our client, Widget Shoes, selling shoes to a customer purchasing 30 pairs of shoes in a bulk sale. That customer will pay for the shoes in one of three ways—the customer will pay for the purchase (i) with cash, (ii) with a promise to pay (accounts receivable), or (iii) with a combination of cash and a promise to pay (part cash and part accounts receivable). Thus, revenue is generally comprised of sales of inventory for cash and sales of inventory for credit (accounts receivable). This is important, because this now tells you that the revenue account does *not* tell you the amount of cash that the corporation has earned from sales. Instead, revenue tells you the inventory sold and paid for with cash as well as the inventory sold and paid for with accounts receivable. The net here is to remember that the amount of revenue that a corporation earned over the fiscal period is *not* equivalent to the amount of cash that the corporation earned over the fiscal period: revenue does not equal cash received.

Cost of Goods Sold—The cost of goods sold (also referred to by its acronym COGS) reflects the costs that the corporation incurred to acquire, manufacture, and produce the inventory the corporation sells. To think of this simply, consider our client, Widget Shoes, and its sales process. Widget Shoes sells shoes to customers, but to have shoes to sell, Widget Shoes must acquire the components to manufacture the shoes. The revenue line on the Income Statement reflects how much Widget earned from selling its inventory of shoes, and the cost of goods sold reflects how much *cost* Widget incurred in acquiring the shoe components and the *costs* of manufacturing these shoes. These costs would include such things as the costs of the rubber for the bottom of the shoes, the costs of the shoelaces and the costs of the metal lace eyelets. There is an entire area of accounting dedicated to determining exactly which costs should be included in costs of goods sold. For example, after many years of teaching this, I *know* some of you are contemplating whether the costs of the air conditioning to cool the factory where the shoes are manufactured should be included or whether the wages paid to the employees to manufacture the shoes should be included, but don't think too deeply about what is included and not; by the time the financial statements will reach your legal desk, this determination has already been made. And, if you truly need to know the answer to this inquiry to address a legal question, this is a question you can easily ask the accountant who prepared the financial statements. So, the takeaway here is to understand that cost of goods sold is the costs the corporation incurred to acquire, manufacture, and produce the inventory and that the specific components of cost of goods sold will be determined by our friendly and experienced accountant.

Gross Profit—Gross Profit is just a calculation: revenue minus cost of goods sold. Simply, Gross Profit tells you how much of the corporation's revenue is consumed by the cost of acquiring the corporation's inventory. Let us assume, for example, that Widget Shoes earns $100,000 in gross revenue from selling shoes and has gross profit of $10,000. That means that $90,000 or ninety percent of the corporation's revenue is spent obtaining the inventory. Given that ninety percent of the corporation's revenue is spent paying for inventory, a natural question is how will Widget have sufficient money to pay for its employees, its utilities, or the costs to lease its operating location? For some companies in certain industries, ninety percent is high and for other industries, it is normal. Either way, gross profit is a good indicator of whether the corporation is making enough off of its inventory to operate profitably. We will discuss more in-depth financial analysis in the Financial Statement Analysis chapter.

2. Expenses

Expenses are the costs a corporation incurs to operate its business.

Operating Expenses often include such costs like utility expenses (every corporation, even the very "green corporations," has to have heat, air and electricity to operate), rental expenses (even those corporations with a small footprint have to have some platform from which to sell the shoes—whether it is online, retail storefront, pop-up malls, or sidewalk sales, there has to be some physical or virtual location and the cost of that location has to be accounted for), and salaries expenses (if Widget Shoes has salespeople selling the shoes in a storefront or online, those employees are required to be paid a wage, and those costs must be reflected in the corporation's expenses).

Depreciation Expense is the amount of depreciation for the fiscal period. Recall the discussion of accumulated depreciation from the Balance Sheet. Depreciation expense is the amount of depreciation for the fiscal period, and accumulated depreciation is the total amount that an asset has been depreciated over the useful life of that asset. In other words, accumulated depreciation is the total amount of the depreciation expense taken over the useful life of that asset.

Amortization Expense is the amount of amortization for the fiscal period. Similar to depreciation, amortization expense is the amount of amortization for the fiscal period, and accumulated amortization is the total amount that a specific asset has been amortized over the useful life of the asset. Just like with depreciation, accumulated amortization is the total amount of the amortization expense taken over the useful life of that asset.

Interest Expense is the corporation's cost of borrowing money. Corporations, like individuals, must pay interest when borrowing money. The cost of borrowing money is determined by the interest rate the lender charges the borrower for borrowing money.

Tax Expense is the amount of income taxes that the corporation paid to federal, state and/or local governments during the fiscal period for the taxable income that the corporation generated. As you know, governments generally do not generate independent revenue, but collect most of its revenue from imposing taxes on entities such as individual workers, property owners, and corporations.

Net Profit is what remains of revenue after all expenses have been accounted for. If you review the sample Income Statement, you will see that, mathematically, net profit is the difference of revenue minus expenses.

B. Capitalizing Costs

Capitalized Assets or Capitalized Costs—As you now know, a corporation's Income Statement shows a corporation's profitability by subtracting a corporation's expenses from the corporation's revenue. As previously stated, the Income Statement is one long equation. Thus, mathematically, a reduction in a corporation's expense results in an increase in a corporation's net profit. What happens to a corporation's net profit in a year when the corporation has a very large expense? Mathematically, the corporation's net profit will also decrease. To help manage such large impacts on a corporation's net profit, sometimes a corporation will *capitalize* an asset—meaning that instead of recording a cost as an expense on the Income Statement, that cost will be recorded as an asset on the Balance Sheet. Yes, yes this is a confusing concept, so bear with me as I give you a more intuitive example.

Let's walk through an example of Widget Shoes purchasing a van. If the corporation purchases the van for $50,000 in cash, the van purchase will be recorded as follows:

Widget Shoes Journal Entries

1/1/2019	Shares	$100,000
	Cash	$100,000
	To record the issuance and sale of $100,000 shares for cash.	
2/1/2019	Rental Expense	$1,000
	Cash	$1,000
	To record rental expense for renting warehouse.	
2/30/2019	Salary Expense	$500
	Cash	$500
	To record salary expense for hiring workers.	
3/01/2019	Property, Plant and Equipment	$40,000 (+)
	Cash	$40,000 (−)

continued

continued

> *To record the purchase of shoe-making equipment (the account balance for property, plant and equipment would increase to reflect the acquisition of the equipment, while the account balance for cash would decrease to reflect the expenditure of cash).*

4/01/2019	Van	$50,000 (+)
	Cash	$50,000 (−)

> *To record the purchase of a van for use by the corporation (the account balance for the new asset, Van, would increase to reflect the acquisition of the van, while the account balance for cash would decrease to reflect the expenditure of cash).*

Let's assume that after nine years, the van's net book value is $5,000 after depreciation. However, because the van is older, Widget Shoes must decide whether to sell the van, retire the van, or repair the van which would extend the van's useful life. After deliberation, Widget Shoes decided to repair the van. The repair costs $20,000 which Widget Shoes estimates would add another five years to the life of the van. If Widget Shoes records the expense of repairing that van, Widget would be recording a $20,000 expense and suffering a corresponding decrease in its net profit. To lessen the impact of such a large expense on a corporation's net profit, GAAP allows companies to "*capitalize*" those expenses. In essence, the corporation is not required to record such an expense on the Income Statement which would decrease net profit by the amount of that expense. Instead, GAAP allows companies to add the amount of that expense to the asset on the Balance Sheet. This results in protecting the corporation's net profit, because large expenses are not recorded on the Income Statement reducing the corporation's net profit. Asset capitalization is a much more complicated concept, but this gives you a broad enough overview to have a general understanding of the concept. To see how capitalizing an expense can impact the Income Statement, consider the following:

Widget Shoes

Without Capitalized Assets:		With Capitalized Assets:	
Revenue	$100,000	Revenue	$100,000
−Cost of Goods Sold	−20,000	−Cost of Goods Sold	−20,000
=Gross Profit	=80,000	=Gross Profit	=80,000
−Rent Expense	−10,000	−Rent Expense	−10,000
−Salary Expense	−10,000	−Salary Expense	−10,000
−*Van Repair Expense*	−20,000	−~~Van Repair Expense~~*	−0
=Net Profit	=40,000	=Net Profit	=60,000

*This $20,000 is instead transferred to the Balance Sheet to increase the book value of the van.

As you can see, capitalizing the van repair expense results in a net profit that is $20,000 higher than it would have been had the corporation not capitalized the expense associated with repairing the van. The WorldCom case study at the end of this chapter provides further evaluation of how this accounting treatment can be used to manipulate a corporation's net profit which, in the case of WorldCom, resulted in significant *legal* consequences for the corporation (all the juicy stuff the law students reading this book find much more intriguing!).

Impairment occurs when the future cash flows that an asset is anticipated to generate are less than the current book value of that asset. To address this, companies can reduce the value of that asset by charging the amount of that reduction to an "Impairment" account on a corporation's Income Statement. This is an advanced accounting concept, but one that is intuitive. Assets are expected to generate future cash flow—for example, inventory is expected to be sold to generate cash, and accounts receivables are expected to be paid to the corporation in cash. So, when the anticipated future cash flows are calculated and anticipated to be less than the current book value of that asset, companies can reduce the book value of such an asset. The Worldcom case study at the end of this chapter demonstrates how a corporation's financial challenges can result in the impairment of assets and how that can impact the Income Statement.

C. Income Statement Interpretation

1. Profitability

The Income Statement tells the users of financial statements how profitable a corporation is over a period of time and helps the user to see where the corporation spent that revenue during the fiscal period. Looking at the Income Statement earlier in this chapter, you see that the corporation's revenue is mostly spent on operating expenses.

2. Net Profit Is Not Net Cash

It is easy to think of the Income Statement as simply a reflection of the amount of money that a corporation earned, then spent in expenses, with net profit as the cash that the corporation has left over. While that is intuitive, there are a few accounts on the Income Statement that prevent this from being true. Remember that revenue is earned when inventory is sold for cash and/or for a promise to pay. Additionally, revenue, depreciation and amortization are accounts that do not reflect actual cash expenditures. Thus, the calculation of net profit is not the calculation of the corporation's net cash.

If a user wants to see how much cash the corporation generated during the fiscal period, the user should look to another financial statement, the Cash Flow Statement.

D. Chapter 3 Income Statement Exercises and Case Studies

Exercise 3.1—Main St. Corp

This exercise is designed to help you become a bit more familiar with the Income Statement by asking you to perform some calculations based on the Income Statement's numbers. As with the Balance Sheet review, these questions are intentionally straight-forward to ease you into financial statement review and analysis. Please note that you will need a calculator to complete this exercise. You do not need a financial calculator; the calculator on your phone will suffice.

At the last meeting of the Widget Shoes Board of Directors ("Board"), the Board approved using some of the net profit from the last fiscal year to purchase stock in another corporation as an investment. The Board passed a Board resolution with investment parameters requiring that the money only be invested in a corporation that meets certain financial requirements. The investment parameters are:

<u>2019–2020 Investment Parameters</u>

1. Cost of goods sold as a percentage of revenue: the cost of goods sold should be no more than 40% of revenue for 2016, 2017 and 2018.
2. Revenue increases: revenue should increase every year by at least 5%.
3. Operating expenses: operating expenses should be no more than 35% of gross profit for 2016, 2017 and 2018.
4. Research and development: the corporation's research and development should be at least 40% of total operating expenses in 2018.
5. Bottom line: the corporation's net income should be at least $45 billion dollars for 2016, 2017, and 2018.

The Board asks you, as their legal counsel, whether an investment in stock of Main St. Corp, Inc. would satisfy the terms of the Board's resolution. The Main St. Corp Income Statement they provided you to review is here:

Main St Corp, Inc.
INCOME STATEMENT
(In millions)

	Years ended		
	September 29, 2018	September 30, 2017	September 24, 2016
Revenue	$265,595	$229,234	$215,639
(less) Cost of goods sold	163,756	141,048	131,376
Gross profit	101,839	88,186	84,263
Operating expenses:			
Research and development	14,236	11,581	10,045
Selling, general and administrative	16,705	15,261	14,194
Total operating expenses	30,941	26,842	24,239
Operating income	70,898	61,344	60,024
Other income/(expense), net	2,005	2,745	1,348
Income before provision for income taxes	72,903	64,089	61,372
Provision for income taxes	13,372	15,738	15,685
Net income	$59,531	$48,351	$45,687

Using the Main St. Corp Income Statement, determine whether an investment in Main St. Corp satisfies the parameters by calculating each parameter for Main St. Corp.

Case Study 3.2—WorldCom, Inc.

This case study will be more complex than the ones we have completed so far. But worry not, you can handle this. This case study further elucidates the lawyer's role in a corporation's business operations and the lawyer's need to understand financial concepts. This case study is about a corporation, WorldCom, Inc., which, at one point, was one of the largest telecommunications companies in the world before a massive financial scandal prompted the corporation's bankruptcy and reorganization. This case study demonstrates the impact of depreciation and amortization on the net profit of a corporation's Income Statement. As you review the case study, consider a lawyer's need to understand financial statement analysis when representing stakeholders in the litigation that followed. Additionally, think about the legal responsibilities that a corporation has—it should present accurate and truthful financial data via its financial statements. This case study also reinforces the business concepts of impairment and capitalized expenses.

Below is a summary of the Income Statement that WorldCom filed with the SEC at the end of fiscal year 2001 (some account names have been renamed or accounts combined for ease of review):

WorldCom, Inc. and Subsidiaries
Consolidated Statement of Operations (In Millions, Except Per Share Data)

	Original Dec. 31, 2000	Restated Dec. 31, 2000	Original Dec. 31, 2001	Restated Dec. 31, 2001
Revenues	$39,090	$39,344	$35,179	$37,668
Operating Expenses:				
Line costs	$15,462		$14,739	
Access costs		$16,903		$16,015
Costs of services and products		$5,092		$5,377
Selling, general and administrative	$10,597	$10,337	$11,046	$10,660
Depreciation and amortization	$4,878	$8,485	$5,880	$4,851
Unclassified (income) expense		$426		($383)
Property, plant and equipment impairment charges		$14,057		$5,729
Goodwill and intangibles impairment charges		$33,123		$6,863
Total Operating Expenses	$30,937	$88,423	$31,665	$49,112
Operating Income (loss)	**$8,153**	**($49,079)**	**$3,514**	**($11,444)**
Other Income (Expense)				
Interest expense	($970)	($1,300)	($1,533)	($2,099)
Miscellaneous	$385	$459	$412	($931)
Reorganization items, net				$0
Income before income taxes, minority interests and cumulative effect of accounting change (Restated as: Loss from continuing operations before income taxes, minority interests and cumulative effect of a change in accounting principle)	$7,568	($49,920)	$2,393	($14,474)
Provision for income taxes (Restated as: Income tax expense (benefit))	$3,025	($1,915)	$927	$503
Income before minority interests and cumulative effect of accounting change	$4,543		$1,466	
Minority Interests	($305)	$358	$35	($702)

continued

continued

Loss from continuing operations before cumulative effect of a change in accounting principle		($48,363)		($14,275)
Net loss from discontinued operations		($449)		($1,323)
Income (Loss) before cumulative effect of accounting change/principle	**$4,238**	**($48,812)**	**$1,501**	**($15,598)**
Cumulative effect of accounting change (net of income tax of $50 in 2000)	($85)			
Cumulative effect of a change in accounting principle		($97)		$1
Net Income (Loss)	**$4,153**	**($48,909)**	**$1,501**	**($15,597)**

To become more familiar with this corporation's financial condition, let us review some highlights in this Income Statement together:

Financial Statement Title—As you see in the Income Statement, some companies refer to their Income Statement as the Statement of Operations.

Consolidated Financial Statements—You may have noticed that this financial statement is titled not only as a Statement of Operations, but as the "Consolidated" Statement of Operations. Consolidated financial statements occur when the financial results of a corporation that has subsidiaries, or a group of companies with single ownership, are presented as a single entity to display the financial results of the corporate group. In this instance, the group of companies that comprise WorldCom, Inc. and its subsidiaries are presented to display their combined financial results.

Restated Financial Statements—As you can see in the Income Statement, there are two sets of financial results for each fiscal period. There are the "Original" and the "Restated" results. On occasion, a corporation finds discrepancies in its previously published financial statements that necessitate the corporation republishing the corrected financial results as 'Restated' financial statements.

Questions for Case Study 3.2—WorldCom

Note that you will need a calculator for this exercise. This exercise is designed to help familiarize you with basic financial statement analysis. The goal of this exercise is to help you become more comfortable analyzing financial statements.

1. Using the Original FYE 2000 and 2001 Income Statements, what is the percentage of revenue growth from FYE 2000 to FYE 2001?

2. Using the Restated FYE 2000 and 2001 Income Statements, what is the percentage of revenue growth from FYE 2000 to FYE 2001?

3. What was the total amount of reduction in net income from the Original 2000 Income Statement to the Restated 2000 Income Statement?

4. What percentage of revenue were Line Costs for the Original Income Statement for fiscal years 2000 and 2001?

5. What percentage of revenue were Access Costs *plus* Costs of Services and Products for the Restated Income Statements for fiscal years 2000 and 2001?

6. What is the total amount of impairment from the Restated FY 2000 and FY 2001 Income Statements for the "Property, plant and equipment impairment charges" account and the "Goodwill and intangibles impairment" account?

7. What is the single biggest financial reason why the corporation's $4.2 billion net income in the original FY 2000 Income Statement plunged to an almost $49 billion net loss in the restated FY 2000 Income Statement?

To provide some background about WorldCom, read the corporation's self-description from an excerpt of the corporation's 2002 10-K filing below. WorldCom described itself as follows:[1]

We are one of the world's leading global communication companies, providing a broad range of communication services in over 200 countries on six continents. Each day, we serve thousands of businesses and government entities throughout the world and provide voice and Internet communication services for millions of consumer customers. We operate one of the most extensive communications networks in the world, comprising approximately 98,000 route miles of network connections linking metropolitan centers and various regions across North America, Europe, Asia, Latin America, the Middle East, Africa and Australia. We own one of the most extensive Internet protocol backbones, and we are one of the largest carriers of international voice traffic.

As you may recall from the WorldCom Statement of Operations, WorldCom issued a Restated Consolidated Statement of Operations. To better understand why WorldCom's financial statements changed so dramatically, let us review excerpts from the Report of Investigation by the Special Investigative Committee of the Board of Directors of WorldCom, Inc. ("Committee"), filed with the Securities and Exchange Commission ("WorldCom Report"). The WorldCom Report states that:

On June 25, 2002, WorldCom announced that it intended to restate its financial statements for 2001 and the first quarter of 2002. It stated that it had determined that certain transfers totaling $3.852 billion during that period from "line cost" expenses (costs of transmitting calls) to asset accounts were not made in accordance with generally accepted accounting principles ("GAAP"). Less than one month later, WorldCom and substantially all of its active U.S.

---

1. WorldCom Form 10-K, Part I, Item I—Business.

subsidiaries filed voluntary petitions for reorganization under Chapter 11 of the Bankruptcy Code. WorldCom subsequently announced that it had discovered an additional $3.831 billion in improperly reported earnings before taxes for 1999, 2000, 2001 and first quarter 2002. It has also written off approximately $80 billion of the stated book value of the assets on the Company's balance sheet at the time the fraud was announced.[2]

As you can imagine, accounting irregularities of this magnitude were significant. The company sought bankruptcy protection. This financial collapse was also reflected in the company's 2002 10-K which stated:

> In June 25, 2002, WorldCom, Inc. and substantially all of its U.S. subsidiaries filed voluntary petitions for relief in the U.S. Bankruptcy Court for the Southern District of New York under Chapter 11 of Title 11 of the U.S. bankruptcy code. We continue to operate our businesses and manage our properties as debtors-in-possession, and we have filed a plan of reorganization with the Bankruptcy Court. On October 31, 2003, the Bankruptcy Court confirmed our plan of reorganization and, subject to certain conditions, we currently expect to emerge from bankruptcy in 2004. Upon emergence, we will change our legal name to MCI, Inc. and will reincorporate as a Delaware corporation."[3]

Questions for Case Study 3.2 cont'd—WorldCom

Consider the following from the perspective of the company's internal legal counsel:

8. When the internal legal counsel first heard of the financial irregularities, can you identify what some of their legal duties might have been?

9. If you are internal legal counsel, what might the Office of General Counsel report to the Board of Directors after OGC becomes aware of the financial irregularities?

10. For those of you who have studied corporate governance law, what are the responsibilities of the Board of Directors?

11. Who are the potential affected parties to such allegations of financial misstatements?

After the financial challenges were discovered, the company's Board of Directors initiated an investigation of the accounting irregularities that led to the company's financial restatements. Review the following excerpts from the WorldCom Report explaining the Committee's findings. Read this as though you are the company's internal legal counsel and try to spot potential legal issues.

---

2. WorldCom Report, p2.
3. WorldCom Form 10-K.

From 1999 until 2002, WorldCom suffered one of the largest public company accounting frauds in history. As enormous as the fraud was, it was accomplished in a relatively mundane way: more than $9 billion in false or unsupported accounting entries were made in WorldCom's financial systems in order to achieve desired reported financial results.[4]

In the 1990s, the principal business strategy of WorldCom's Chief Executive Officer, Bernard J. Ebbers, was growth through acquisitions. The currency for much of that strategy was WorldCom stock, and the success of the strategy depended on a consistently increasing stock price. WorldCom pursued scores of increasingly large acquisitions. The strategy reached its apex with WorldCom's acquisition in 1998 of MCI Communications Corporation ("MCI"), a company more than two-and-a-half times WorldCom's size (by revenues). Ebbers' acquisition strategy largely came to an end by early 2000 when WorldCom was forced to abandon a proposed merger with Sprint Corporation because of antitrust objections.[5]

A. The Nature of the Accounting Fraud

WorldCom's improper accounting took two principal forms: reduction of reported line costs, WorldCom's largest category of expenses; and exaggeration of reported revenues. The overall objective of these efforts was to hold reported line costs to approximately 42% of revenues (when in fact they typically reached levels in excess of 50%), and to continue reporting double-digit revenue growth when actual growth rates were generally substantially lower.

1. Reduction of Reported Line Costs

WorldCom initially discovered, and announced, that its financial personnel had improperly transferred $3.852 billion from line cost expenses to asset accounts during 2001 and the first quarter of 2002. Later WorldCom announced additional line cost accounting irregularities that, when combined with the first announcement, totaled $6.412 billion in improper reductions to line costs. In addition to the accounting irregularities disclosed, we have identified other manipulations of line costs. In total, from the second quarter of 1999 through the first quarter of 2002, WorldCom improperly reduced its reported line costs (and increased pre-tax income) by over $7 billion.

---

4. Report of Investigation by the Special Investigative Committee of the Board of Directors of WorldCom, Inc., Mar 31, 2003, pg 1.

5. *Id.*

continued

continued

The improper line cost adjustments included, first, releases of accruals in 1999 and 2000; then, when there were no more large accruals available to release, capitalization of operating line costs in 2001 and early 2002.

Line costs are the costs of carrying a voice call or data transmission from its starting point to its ending point. They are WorldCom's largest single expense: from 1999 to 2001, line costs accounted for approximately half of the Company's total expenses. As a result, WorldCom management and outside analysts paid particular attention to line cost levels and trends. One key measure of performance both within WorldCom and in communications with the public was the ratio of line cost expense to revenue (the "line cost E/R ratio").[6]

Thereafter, from the first quarter of 2001 through the first quarter of 2002, WorldCom improperly reduced its reported line costs by $3.8 billion, principally by capitalizing $3.5 billion of line costs—at Sullivan's direction—in violation of WorldCom's capitalization policy and well-established accounting standards. The line costs that WorldCom capitalized were ongoing, operating expenses that accounting rules required WorldCom to recognize immediately.[7]

By capitalizing operating expenses, WorldCom shifted these costs from its income statement to its balance sheet and increased its reported pre-tax income and earnings per share. Had WorldCom not capitalized these expenses, it would have reported a pre-tax loss in three of the five quarters in which the improper capitalization entries occurred. [In the second quarter of 2001, WorldCom reported pre-tax income of $159 million. If WorldCom had not improperly capitalized $560 million in operating line costs for that quarter, however, the Company would have reported a $401 million pre-tax loss. For the fourth quarter of 2001, WorldCom reported pre-tax income of $401 million instead of a pre-tax loss of $440 million because it capitalized $841 million of line costs. Similarly, the improper capitalization of $818 million in line costs for the first quarter of 2002 allowed WorldCom to report pre-tax income of $240 million instead of a $578 million pre-tax loss. For purposes of this analysis, we do not attempt to correct the effects of other accounting irregularities (such as improper accrual releases) discussed in this Report.][8]

---

6. *Id.* at p 9–10.
7. *Id.*
8. *Id.*

Case Study 3.3—WorldCom Insider's View

Now that you have reviewed the financial statements and considered the attorney's role, read the excerpt below from an interview with Dennis Beresford to better understand what happened behind the scenes. After Worldcom's Board of Directors ("Board") discovered the financial reporting fraud, Worldcom's Board decided to invite new members to join the Board to assist in an independent investigation ("Investigation") of the fraud. Beresford said he joined the Board in July 2001 to help lead the Investigation.[9] While Beresford said he thought the investigation would be "pretty scary" given its scope, since Beresford's background is in auditing and financial reporting, he said he also found it intriguing because it looked like it might be "the largest financial reporting fraud in history, which it turned out to be."[10] Beresford joined the Board and said that he became the chairman of the Board's Audit Committee and, along with two other new members, formed the Special Investigation Committee overseeing the work of the company's outside law firm conducting the investigation.[11]

According to Beresford, the Board learned about the fraud from the Director of Internal Audit who had identified some financial irregularities in conjunction with the company's outside auditors.[12] According to Beresford, while the financial fraud was very complex, he describes it this way:

> the so-called line costs were the expenses that the company paid to have other companies carry their long distance calls on their systems. So, without getting very technical, if you were calling from Chicago to somebody in, lets say, Honolulu, the call goes across a number of systems, different lines and so forth, maybe it goes through the air these days; but at least in those days a lot of times it would go through different wires and things like that. And it might go from the Chicago telephone company to the Midwest telephone company to the pacific coast telephone company to the Hawaii telephone company. Some of those are real big companies, some of them are regional companies, some of them are small companies. And, the total cost of that call might be a dollar, but, the companies that the system that carries that call is not all owned by the same company. So, some company owns the part of the system that originates the call, somebody else owns the part of the system that gets the call from Chicago to, lets say, Denver, somebody else owns the part of the system that gets the call from Denver to San Francisco, and somebody else owns that part from San Francisco to Honolulu.

---

9. Interview on June 4, 2020 with Dennis Beresford, Former Board of Director member for Worldcom. Transcript on file with author.

10. *Id.*

11. *Id.*

12. *Id.*

So, of that dollar then, basically what has to happen is that the amount gets split up....

With generally accepted accounting principles, in a manufacturing company its sort of like the cost of goods sold. You have a product you sell and it costs you something to produce that product. In this particular case you have the product, which is the telephone call that you're selling to somebody and the cost is principally your own system plus the amounts that you had to pay to use other people's systems. So those costs that you're incurring to pay the company out in Denver and the company out in San Francisco and the company out Hawaii, would all be treated as current period expenses. But what World-Com was doing, instead of treating them as expenses, they were capitalizing them, and they were treating them as assets. They were pretending as though those amounts instead of being treated as a current period expense, would be considered part of their property, plant, and equipment.

So, it was, you might say the world's simplest accounting fraud, in terms of how they actually did it. But, it was hard to tell if you just took a cursory look at their financial statements because their operating ratio of line costs, or cost of goods sold, to revenues looked fairly comparable to what it had been in the past. The problem was they were going through a period of time when there was a lot more competition and their cost of goods sold, their line costs, should have been an increasing percentage of their revenues, and, in fact, they weren't. They were staying about the same as they had been historically. So, they were achieving that by falsifying the accounting.[13]

As you can see from the WorldCom Report and the Beresford interview, using capitalized costs is a way to reduce expenses and thus improve a company's net income. But, improperly categorizing expenses creates financial and legal consequences including hiding actual financial losses, which as a lawyer should raise legal issues such as potentially violating securities regulations laws, potential litigation from shareholders from loss of shareholder value, and litigation from others negatively impacted by the financial misrepresentations.

It is helpful to think about what the lawyer's role should be in this context. Beresford notes the importance "for business lawyers to have an understanding of business or to have a business background."[14] When asked about what makes a good business lawyer, Beresford responded that it's helpful to have enough of an understanding of the company's products, the company's manufacturing processes and the company's major risks. He notes that that good business lawyers should be more than a "textbook lawyer."[15] In his experience, he says that "the best general counsels

---

13. *Id.*
14. *Id.*
15. *Id.*

that I've seen have been the ones who the CEO considers to be his or her advisor" with "terrific judgment" while keeping in mind the bigger picture of the implications of a decision on stakeholder or community relations.[16]

Chapter 3 Highlights

- The Income Statement shows you a corporation's revenue and expenses.
- It also shows you a corporation's profitability, not a corporation's liquidity.
- The balances on the Income Statement are cumulative.
- Remember that net profit does not equal net cash.
- Companies can impact their net income by capitalizing expenses.

---

16. *Id.*

Four

Cash Flow Statement

- This chapter will cover the Cash Flow Statement, the third of four major financial statements, and explain how to use it as an evaluative tool to demonstrate a corporation's generation and use of cash.

- While you have learned that the Income Statement reflects the revenue that a corporation has generated over a fiscal period, you will now learn how the Cash Flow Statement reflects how the corporation earned cash and how the corporation spent that cash.

- The Cash Flow Statement is intuitively titled, as it does just that—it shows a corporation's cash inflow and a corporation's cash outflow. While the Income Statement shows a corporation's *profitability*, the Cash Flow Statement shows a corporation's *cash flow*. As you recall from the previous chapter, a corporation's net profit *does not* equal a corporation's net cash flow, and after reviewing this chapter, you will see the difference between a corporation's cash flow and a corporation's profitability.

- This chapter will also cover how the Cash Flow Statement can demonstrate whether a corporate client is in compliance with its financial obligations.

A. Income Statement vs. Cash Flow Statement

As you now know, the Income Statement tells you about a corporation's profitability. For a quick review, remember that a corporation's:

- Balance Sheet tells you—

  what a corporation owns and owes, how much a corporation's owners have contributed to the corporation and an approximation of how much profit the corporation has retained in the corporation.

- Income Statement tells you—

  a corporation's revenue and expenses resulting in a corporation's net profit. However, because companies can reduce their net profit by depreciation expense and amortization expense (remember those?), which are *non-cash deductions,* a corporation's net profit **is not** the same as a corporation's net cash.

Given that, how do you determine a corporation's net cash inflow and outflow for the fiscal period? This is the beauty of the Cash Flow Statement as it answers one of the most important questions companies want answered—how did the corporation generate its cash flow and on what did the corporation expend its cash? Once you understand this basic principle, the Cash Flow Statement should be relatively intuitive.

B. Cash Flow Statement Overview

The Cash Flow Statement, like the Income Statement, is one long mathematical equation. It starts with a corporation's:

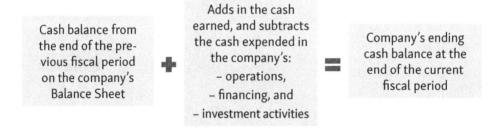

That's it. One long mathematical equation. To state it more plainly, the Cash Flow Statement answers how the corporation's cash balance from the end of the previous fiscal period resulted in the cash balance at the end of the corporation's current fiscal period. To put it simply, the Cash Flow Statement tells a story of how the corporation earned its cash and how it spent it.

Generally, a for-profit corporation's main business is the manufacture or purchase of inventory or services and the sale of that inventory or service for a cash profit. That corporation must generate or obtain cash to purchase the corporation's inventory, pay its operating expenses like salaries and rent, purchase or rent the corporation's property, plant and equipment to conduct its operations, and return profits to its owners. Those activities are cash activities. So, when you think about these financial transactions, it's easy to lump them into three major categories—

- Cash Flow from Operations,
- Cash Flow from Financing, and
- Cash Flow from Investments.

Operations—Let's start with Operations. This one is intuitive, as it's easy to visualize the operations of a corporation. Let's consider our company, Widget Shoes. What are the operations of Widget Shoes? Its operations include the manufacture and sale of its shoes, including paying vendors for the shoe components, paying the salaries of employees to operate the business, paying the cost of repairs for its van, and paying the other costs related to the manufacture and sale of its shoes.

Financing—Now, let's think about Financing. This one is also relatively intuitive. Financing would refer to how Widget Shoes finances its operations. Since Widget Shoes needs cash for its operations, where does Widget Shoes get this cash? If the company is operating well, Widget Shoes will generate its cash from its operations—the sale of its inventory. If the company determines that it needs additional cash beyond that generated from its operations, the company may seek financing in the form of debt—such as a loan, or equity—such as the sale of preferred or common stock. These activities are considered "financing" activities. If you are wondering how debt financing and equity financing are cash activities, think about what happens when you take out a student loan. The lender provides you cash…well, ok, yes, the lender provides cash to the law school on your behalf…but, nevertheless, the loan generates cash. So, for those of you who are borrowing to pay for law school, in industry parlance, you are "financing" your education. Similarly, with equity, if Widget Shoes sells common stock to an investor, the investor receives common stock in Widget Shoes and Widget Shoes receives cash from the investor. Thus, borrowing debt or selling equity generates cash and are thus "financing" activities.

Investing—Finally, let's move onto Investing. This one is less intuitive and badly named. Admittedly, when you hear the term "Investing," one generally thinks about investing in the stock market, investing in mutual funds, or investing in money markets. It is understandable that your initial thought of "investing" was your friends and family members imploring you to "invest well" or to make sure you "invest" your money. Investment often means the purchase of a financial security with the goal of earning a profit from that purchase. So, you are in good company when you think that the sale of common stock intuitively would be a part of "investing." *However,* just to make learning this material that much more fun for you, Investing on the Cash Flow Statement means something different. Here, it actually refers to long-term capital investments by the corporation such as the purchase and sale of property, plant and equipment.

Now that you have a fundamental grip on these three categories, review the previous Cash Flow Statement again as it should make a bit more sense now. The Cash Flow Statement starts with the corporation's cash balance at the end of the previous fiscal period, adds in the net cash flow from the corporation's operating activities, adds in the net cash flow from the corporation's financing activities, and then adds in the net cash flow from the corporation's investing activities to arrive at the cash balance at the end of the corporation's current fiscal period. For those of you who are more comfortable with this in equation form, the Cash Flow Statement formula for Widget Shoes for December 31, 2020, would look like this:

Cash Balance on December 31, 2019

+/– Cash flow from Operating Activities during fiscal year 2020

+/– Cash flow from Financing Activities during fiscal year 2020

+/– Cash flow from Investing Activities during fiscal year 2020

= Cash Balance on December 31, 2020

Now, let's see how well we understand this concept by working through some questions using a Cash Flow Statement from Main Street Shoes, a much larger shoe corporation.

Main St. Shoes—Consolidated Statement of Cash Flows (in millions)

	Years ended		
	Sept 26, 2015	Sept 27, 2014	Sept 28, 2013
Cash and cash equivalents, beginning of the year	$13,844	$14,259	$10,746
Operating activities:			
Net income	53,394	39,510	37,037
Adjustments to reconcile net income to cash generated by operating activities:			
Depreciation and amortization	11,257	7,946	6,757
Share-based compensation expense	3,586	2,863	2,253
Deferred income tax expense	1,382	2,347	1,141

Changes in operating assets and liabilities:

Accounts receivable, net	611	(4,232)	(2,172)
Inventories	(238)	(76)	(973)
Vendor non-trade receivables	(3,735)	(2,220)	223
Other current and non-current assets	(179)	167	1,080
Accounts payable	5,400	5,938	2,340
Deferred revenue	1,042	1,460	1,459
Other current and non-current liabilities	8,746	6,010	4,521
Cash generated by operating activities	81,266	59,713	53,666

Investing activities:

Purchases of marketable securities	(166,402)	(217,128)	(148,489)
Proceeds from maturities of marketable securities	14,538	18,810	20,317
Proceeds from sales of marketable securities	107,447	189,301	104,130
Payments made in connection with business acquisitions, net	(343)	(3,765)	(496)
Payments for acquisition of property, plant and equipment	(11,247)	(9,571)	(8,165)
Payments for acquisition of intangible assets	(241)	(242)	(911)
Other	(26)	16	(160)
Cash used in investing activities	(56,274)	(22,579)	(33,774)

Financing activities:

Proceeds from issuance of common stock	543	730	530
Excess tax benefits from equity awards	749	739	701
Taxes paid related to net share settlement of equity awards	(1,499)	(1,158)	(1,082)
Dividends and dividend equivalents paid	(11,561)	(11,126)	(10,564)
Repurchase of common stock	(35,253)	(45,000)	(22,860)
Proceeds from issuance of term debt, net	27,114	11,960	16,896
Change in commercial paper, net	2,191	6,306	0
Cash used in financing activities	(17,716)	(37,549)	(16,379)

Increase/(decrease) in cash and cash equivalents	7,276	(415)	3,513
Cash and cash equivalents, end of the year	$21,120	$13,844	$14,259

C. Chapter 4 Cash Flow Statement Exercises and Case Studies

Exercise 4.1—Cash Flow Statement Review

This exercise is another straightforward exercise to help familiarize you with the Cash Flow Statement.

1. Assume that your client is a shareholder in the corporation. The client asks you to determine whether Main Street Shoes returned the corporation's cash to its shareholders by repurchasing shares and declaring dividends. In what section on the Cash Flow Statement would you look?

2. To respond to your client's requests for information in the above request, determine the following information:

    a. How much cash did Main Street expend, if any, repurchasing common stock in fiscal year 2013?

    b. How much cash did Main Street expend, if any, for dividends and dividend equivalents in fiscal year 2014?

    c. How much cash did Main Street expend, if any, repurchasing common stock and issuing dividends and dividend equivalents in fiscal year 2015?

    d. How much cash did Main Street expend, if any, repurchasing common stock during fiscal years 2013, 2014, and 2015?

    e. How much cash and cash equivalents did Main Street have at the end of fiscal year 2014?

    f. How much cash and cash equivalents did Main Street have at the end of fiscal year 2015?

    g. How much cash did Main Street expend for business acquisitions during FY 2014?

Case Study 4.2—Carl Icahn Open Letter to Apple Shareholders

On January 23, 2014, one of Apple's then largest shareholders, Carl Icahn, issued an open letter to Apple shareholders arguing that Apple should return more of Apple's cash to Apple shareholders. Think about the discussion in earlier chapters about the purpose of a corporation. If a corporation has cash that it *can* return to its owners, *should* that corporation return that cash to shareholders? How much of a corporation's cash should be retained by the corporation and how much should be returned to the shareholders? This case study provides an example of the tensions that can arise between a corporation with cash and a shareholder who seeks more of that cash returned to shareholders. Below are excerpts from Mr. Icahn's letter:[1]

---

1. Copyright license on file with author.

CARL C. ICAHN
767 Fifth Avenue, 47th Floor
New York, New York 10153

January 23, 2014

Dear Fellow Apple Shareholders,

Over the course of my long career as an investor and as Chairman of Icahn Enterprises, our best performing investments result from opportunities that we like to call "no brainers." Recent examples of such "no brainers" have been our investments in Netflix, Hain Celestial, Chesapeake, Forest Labs and Herbalife, just to name a few. In our opinion, a great example of a "no brainer" in today's market is Apple.... Tim Cook himself has expressed on more than one occasion that Apple is undervalued, and as the company states, it already has in place "the largest share repurchase authorization in history." We believe, however, that this share repurchase authorization can and should be even larger, and effectuating that for the benefit of all of the company's shareholders is the sole intention of our proposal. The company has recommended voting against our proposal for various reasons. It seems to us that the basis of its argument against our proposal is that the company believes, because of the "dynamic competitive landscape" and because its "rapid pace of innovation require[s] unprecedented investment, flexibility and access to resources", it does not currently have enough excess liquidity to increase the size of its repurchase program. Assuming this indeed is the basis for the company's argument, we find its position overly conservative (almost to the point of being irrational), when we consider that the company had $130 billion of net cash as of September 28, 2013 and that consensus earnings are expected to be almost $40 billion next year. Given this massive net cash position and robust earnings generation, Apple is perhaps the most overcapitalized company in corporate history, from our perspective. Regardless of what liquidity it may require with respect to "unprecedented investment, flexibility and access to resources" for innovation moving forward, we believe the unprecedented degree to which the company is currently overcapitalized would overcompensate for any such investments (including possible investments in strategic M&A, to which the company does not refer). Said another way, we believe that the combination of the company's unprecedentedly enormous net cash balance, robust annual earnings, and tremendous borrowing capacity provide more than enough excess liquidity to afford both the use of cash for any necessary ongoing business-related investments in addition to the cash used for the increased share repurchases proposed.

It is our belief that it is the responsibility of the Board, on behalf of the company's shareholders, to take advantage of such a large and unmistakable opportunity. Indeed, we believe that by choosing not to increase the size of the repurchase program, the directors are actually performing a great disservice to the owners, especially smaller shareholders who may not be in a position to buy more stock themselves. Meanwhile, we are in a position to continue buying shares in the market at today's price, so perhaps we should thank the Board for not being more aggressive, and thus allowing us to accumulate an even larger investment position at a price that reflects the aforementioned valuation disconnect. In fact, over the past two weeks we purchased $1 billion more in Apple shares, $500 million of which we purchased today, bringing our total ownership position in Apple to a current value of approximately $3.6 billion....

In this letter, we have above summarized why we believe Apple is undervalued in order to express how ridiculous it seems to us for Apple to horde so much cash rather than repurchase stock (and thereby use that cash to make a larger investment in itself for the benefit of all of the company's shareholders). In its statement in opposition to our proposal, the company claims that "the Board and management team have demonstrated a strong commitment to returning capital to shareholders" and we believe that is true, but we also believe that commitment is not strong enough given the unique degree to which the company is both undervalued and overcapitalized. Furthermore, it is important to note that a share repurchase is not simply an act of "returning capital to shareholders" since it is also the company effectively making an investment in itself. To us, as long term investors, this is an important difference: a dividend is a pure return of capital while a share repurchase is the company making an investment in itself by buying shares in the market at the current price, which we believe to be undervalued, from shareholders willing to sell at that price for the benefit of shareholders who choose to remain investors for the longer term. And we are long term investors. It should be noted that no one on the Board seems to be an expert in the world of investment management. However, based on our record, we believe few will argue that we are experts in this area, and we have no doubts that the Board is doing a great disservice to its shareholders by not immediately increasing the size of the share repurchase program in order to more effectively take advantage of what we believe to be the company's low market valuation.

We have expressed above what we believe to be the company's primary reason for not supporting our proposal. Conversely, it is our belief that Apple's current excess liquidity is without historical precedent and beyond reasonable comparison to its peers or otherwise, and such dramatic overcapitalization affords the company enough excess liquidity to repurchase the amount of shares we proposed. Apple's existing capital return program has just $37 billion remaining, and the company has until the end of 2015 to complete it. Without any changes to the program, the largest pile of corporate cash in the world is likely to grow even larger, and if the share price rises, this Board will have missed a great opportunity to use more of that hoarded cash to repurchase shares at an attractive value. While it is important for the Board to focus on the return of capital on a sustained basis, it is also important for the

Board to evaluate whether or not its share price is undervalued and to take advantage of it with share repurchases, especially when the balance sheet exhibits dramatic excess liquidity, as we believe Apple's does today....

The company has stated that it is "updating perspectives on its capital return program for 2014 and beyond" and "collecting input from a very broad base of shareholders." We believe, if our proposal receives majority shareholder support, that the Board should respect it and increase the repurchase program as requested. We believe this action will greatly enhance value for all long term shareholders who believe, as we do, in the great potential of this company. If the Board takes this action, we will applaud them for taking advantage of one of the greatest examples of a "no brainer" we have seen in five decades of successful investing.

Sincerely yours,

Carl C. Icahn

Questions for Case Study 4.2 for Class Discussion

1. What do you think was meant by "excess liquidity" as stated in the proposal?
2. What are some business reasons why a corporation like Apple might maintain a large cash balance?
3. The proposal references "share repurchase." What is meant by that? How might an Apple share repurchase impact a shareholder's finances?
4. What is the difference between a company declaring a dividend and repurchasing shares?

Follow-Up

According to an article published in the New York Times, Mr. Icahn ultimately dropped his proposal, stating "we see no reason to persist with our non-binding proposal, especially when the company is already so close to fulfilling our requested repurchase target." Michael J. de la Merced, *Icahn Ends Call for Apple Stock Buyback*, N.Y. Times, Feb 10, 2014.

Chapter 4 Highlights

- The Cash Flow Statement tells you where the corporation generated its cash and where the corporation expended its cash.
- The Cash Flow Statement is separated into the following major sections:
  - Cash Flow from Operations
    - This includes cash flow generated and expended in the corporation's day to day operations.
  - Cash Flow from Financing
    - This includes cash flow generated and expended in obtaining capital for the corporation.
  - Cash Flow from Investments
    - This includes cash flow generated and expended in the corporation's major investments, including in property, plant and equipment.

Five

Financial Statement Analysis

- While the previous chapters provide analysis on reading the major financial statements, this chapter will help you understand how to use financial ratios to analyze those financial statements.

- You will learn how these ratios are useful tools for lawyers to identify trends in a corporate client's financial performance including liquidity, profitability, capitalization, and operational efficiency.

- This chapter also will explain how these trends are useful in evaluating a client's capacity for meeting its legal obligations such as paying employee wages earned, repaying loans and bonds, and maintaining liquidity and profitability minimum requirements.

A. Financial Statement Analysis

Financial statement analysis facilitates the interpretation of the numbers on financial statements. For example, if a financial statement shows that a corporation has $1,000,000 in revenue and $300,000 in net profit, is that good financial performance? How does the corporation determine whether its inventory costs or rent expenses are too high compared to the corporation's competitors? Financial statement analysis enables a user to decipher a corporation's financial performance by comparing relationships between financial statement accounts, reviewing the corporation's performance over a period of time, and comparing a corporation's financial performance against the financial performance of other companies within the same industry or sector.

1. Ratio Analysis

Ratio analysis uses financial ratios to quickly analyze a corporation's financial performance. For example, if a review of the Income Statement shows that the corporation generated revenue of $1,000,000 and cost of goods sold of $800,000, those absolute numbers are most useful when presented in comparison to the corporation's revenue and cost of goods sold in previous years, when presented in comparison to the revenue and cost of goods sold of other similar companies in the same fiscal year, and when presented in comparison to other account balances on the corporation's financial statements. For example, the amount of cost of goods sold is most useful when compared to the amount of revenue the corporation generated during that same fiscal period. So, instead of simply noting cost of goods sold of $800,000, it is more telling to know that of the $1,000,000 that the corporation generated in revenue, $800,000 of that was costs of goods sold expended acquiring or manufacturing the corporation's inventory. In other words, the corporation's cost of goods sold was 80% of the corporation's revenue. That "80%" gives us context to determine whether $800,000 was a positive or negative indicator of financial performance. Using these types of ratios also allows us to easily compare a corporation's financial performance to another corporation's financial performance.

It is important to understand that there is no single list of "correct" financial analysis ratios. Different users use different ratios to determine information most important to them. For example, if your client is seeking a loan from a lender, the lender might be more interested in your client's cash flow ratios to help determine whether there is sufficient cash flow to repay the loan. If your client is an investor looking to invest in a corporation, your client might be more interested in the debt to equity ratio analyzing the amount of debt that the corporation has taken on compared to the amount of equity invested in the corporation. If your corporate client is considering acquiring another corporation, your client might be more interested in a liquidity ratio to determine whether the acquired corporation will have sufficient liquidity throughout the first couple of years after the acquisition.

Below are some of the more common financial ratios:

Table of Financial Ratios

Name of Financial Ratio	Formula of Financial Ratio	Interpretive Guide
Liquidity Ratios		
Working Capital	Current Assets – Current Liabilities	Least conservative analysis of liquidity.
Current Ratio	Current Assets Current Liabilities	Working Capital simply provides an absolute number, whereas the Current Ratio is a specific ratio which permits a clearer analysis.
Quick Ratio	(Cash + Marketable Securities + Short-Term Investments + Receivables) Current Liabilities	Removes non-liquid assets like other assets and inventory, so the Quick Ratio is a more conservative liquidity analysis.
Cash Ratio	(Cash + Marketable Securities + Short-Term Investments) Current Liabilities	Most conservative analysis of liquidity, since all current assets other than the most highly liquid are removed.
Profitability Ratios		
Gross Profit Margin	Gross Profit Revenue	Helps to determine the percentage of revenue that the corporation expends for its inventory.
Operating Profit Margin	Operating Profit Revenue	Helps to determine the percentage of revenue that the corporation expends for its inventory and operating expenses.
Net Profit Margin	Net Profit Revenue	Helps to determine the percentage of revenue that remains after the corporation pays for all of its expenses.
Return on Total Capital	Net Profit + Interest Expense Average Total Capital	Helps to determine the rate of return on a corporation's earnings to the corporation's capital (all equity and debt).
Return on Equity ("ROE")	Net Profit Average Total Equity	Tells the user the return on the total equity invested in a corporation, including common stock and preferred stock.
Return on Owner's Equity	(Net Profit – Preferred Dividend) Average Total Equity	For those interested in the return on equity excluding any dividends paid or owed to preferred stockholders.

continued

continued

Debt Ratios

Debt to Equity Ratio	Total Long-Term Debt Total Equity	This is a capitalization formula. Tells the user the proportion of debt to the total amount of equity, including common and preferred stock.
Debt to Total Capital Ratio	Total Long-Term Debt Total Capital	Shows the proportion of total capital derived from long-term debt. Total Capital includes all debt and all equity.

Cash Flow Ratios

Interest Coverage Ratio	(Net Profit + Tax Expense + Interest Expense) Interest Expense	This helps the user understand the ratio of earnings to the amount of interest expense the corporation must pay. Since Tax Expense and Interest Expense are deducted to calculate Net Profit, those are added back in to calculate the earnings available to pay the interest expense.
Debt Service Coverage Ratio	Net Operating Income Debt Service (Principal Payments)	Helps to determine the ratio of available cash flow (net income less non-cash items such as depreciation expense, amortization expense and non-recurring charges) to the amount of principal payments owed by the corporation.

Legal Highlights

Loan Agreements

Loan agreements often have covenants requiring the corporation to maintain certain financial metrics. Financial ratios allow lawyers to easily determine whether a client is in compliance with those covenants. For example, a corporate loan agreement might require the corporation to have a minimum debt service coverage ratio of 1.25 for the duration of the loan. Or the loan agreement might require your corporate client to maintain a working capital ratio of at least 1.2.

Understanding these ratios can help you advise a client on the potential legal risks of entering into, or not complying with, a loan agreement.

2. Trends

How do you know whether your corporate client's revenues are growing or whether those revenues are stagnant? How do you know whether your client's cash flow is increasing at the rate required by your client's equity investors? When reviewing financial statements, it is important to view them over a period of years—three is a good minimum, five is better. Think about your decision to attend law school. You likely reviewed the rankings for law schools to help you evaluate where to apply based upon your LSAT score and maybe even the weather for those of us teaching in Chicago. If you only looked at the school ranking for the current year, that does not give you sufficient information to determine whether the law school's ranking is increasing, stable or plummeting—a fact, I would think, you would want to know. So, you likely looked at the law school's current ranking and the ranking for the past couple of years to get a better picture of the law school's viability as an educational option for you. That same theory holds for reviewing financial statements, particularly if you are using the financial statements to project the corporation's future financial trends.

B. Chapter 5 Financial Statement Analysis Exercises and Case Studies

Exercise 5.1—Financial Statement Analysis

Review the below Income Statement for an apartment building. What, if anything, can you identify about the corporation's financial condition? Are there any line-items that are problematic? Can you tell whether the corporation's revenue is strong?

Income Statement
2018

Gross Rental Income	$117,000
Vacancies	$(2,000)
Other Income	$860
Total Revenue	$115,860

Expenses	
Accounting	$50
Bad Debts	$–
Cleaning	$2,565
Decorating	$16,046

continued

continued

Electric Bill	$5,000
Extermination	$5,545
Gas Bill	$7,500
Grounds & Misc.	$1,060
HVAC	$–
Insurance	$6,116
Leasing Marketing	
Legal Fees	$2,000
Management Fee	$9,312
Office Supplies	$569
On-site Representative	$8,940
Phone	$851
Repairs	$32,721
Security	$8,270
Snow Removal	$635
Taxes & Licenses	$2,159
Trash removal	$2,099
Water & Sewer Bill	$10,938
Total Expenses:	$122,376
Net Operating Income	$(6,516)
Mortgage	$–
Net Cash Flow	$(6,516)

You likely noticed that the corporation's net cash flow is negative. This certainly indicates a potential problem. Now, look at the corporation's five-year historical financial statement and note whether there are any additional areas of concern. When reviewing the 5-year numbers, compare line items across years to notice trends or anomalies.

Income Statement

	2015	2016	2017	2018	2019
Gross Rental Income	$113,000	$114,000	$115,000	$117,000	$118,000
Vacancies	$(4,094)	$(8,299)	$(11,168)	$(2,000)	$(15,000)
Other Income	$4,102	$2,523	$1,041	$860	$3,498
Total Revenue	$113,008	$108,224	$104,873	$115,860	$106,498

Expenses					
Accounting	$1,200	$1,200	$–	$50	$2,600
Bad Debts	$–	$1,782	$–	$–	
Cleaning	$2,442	$3,320	$2,040	$2,565	$3,100
Decorating		$510	$–	$16,046	$1,340
Electric Bill	$2,216	$1,871	$1,660	$5,000	$2,270
Extermination	$883	$607	$5,153	$5,545	$600
Gas Bill	$8,542	$9,726	$6,861	$7,500	$15,000
Grounds & Misc.	$661	$565	$567	$1,060	$1,800
HVAC	$2,953	$2,503	$5,884	$–	$3,151
Insurance	$4,928	$5,348	$5,162	$6,116	$7,451
Leasing Marketing	$119	$–	$–		
Legal Fees	$657	$985	$419	$2,000	$439
Management Fee	$8,400	$9,043	$9,182	$9,312	$9,913
Office Supplies	$289	$1,799	$1,839	$569	$697
On-site Representative	$900	$100	$4,200	$8,940	$5,940
Phone	$184	$139	$1,603	$851	$929
Repairs	$8,200	$9,187	$16,838	$32,721	$3,426
Security	$–		$–	$8,270	
Snow Removal	$121	$235	$–	$635	$250
Taxes & Licenses	$4,483	$4,762	$2,623	$2,159	$11,021
Trash removal	$2,649	$2,427	$2,242	$2,099	$3,023
Water & Sewer Bill	$2,944	$4,629	$12,133	$10,938	$7,827
Total Expenses:	$52,771	$60,738	$78,406	$122,376	$80,777
Net Operating Income	$60,237	$47,486	$26,467	$(6,516)	$25,721
Mortgage	$20,000	$20,000	$20,000	$–	$–
Net Cash Flow	$40,237	$27,486	$6,467	$(6,516)	$25,721

Now that you see a fuller picture with five years instead of just one, highlight any areas of concern. As you can see, the apartment's vacancies looked relatively harmless amounting to less than 2% of total Gross Rental Income in year 2018. But when you review five years of financial statements, you see that the $2,000 in vacancies in year 2018 was simply an aberration because the corporation has been trending to higher annual vacancies each year.

Calculate the percent of Gross Rental Income that vacancies represent for each year and note the trend.

Legal Highlights

Financial Statement Analysis

When evaluating financial statements, we should look for irregularities or oddities that may indicate a legal risk.

For example, looking at the Income Statement in Exercise 5.1, did you notice in 2018 that the mortgage payment was zero? Is that a potential legal issue? As an attorney, I would confirm that the non-payment was because the loan was repaid in full. It certainly is possible that the client simply stopped paying the mortgage. If that occurred, as lawyers, we would need to review the mortgage loan agreement and determine whether that non-payment is a breach of the mortgage loan agreement and, if so, to advise the client of the potential legal consequences of such a breach.

Simply because we question an item on a financial statement does not automatically make it a legal problem. However, we can only identify legal issues if we, as attorneys, are willing to ask questions.

C. Financial Statement Footnotes

For anyone who has ever read a law review article, you know well an academic's love of footnotes! While they are indeed plentiful, they also contain useful information. The same is true for financial statements. When reviewing corporate financial statements, you may have a question about what you see in the financial statements. The footnotes are often very helpful in explaining changes in trends, account balances, or new line items.

Chapter 5 Highlights

- The Balance Sheet tells you a corporation's liquidity, so many of the most commonly used financial ratios for the Balance Sheet are analyzing the corporation's ability to meet its short- and long-term liabilities with the corporation's short- and long-term assets.
- The Income Statement tells you a corporation's profitability, so many of the most used financial ratios for the Income Statement are analyzing the corporation's profit margins, including the "gross profit margin," the "operating profit margin," and the "net profit margin."

- When analyzing a corporation's financial statements, it is helpful to review a corporation's financial performance over a period of years to identify any changes in trends.

- The footnotes in a corporation's financial statements often provide information helpful in interpreting changes in the corporation's financial statements.

Six

Time Value of Money

- This chapter will introduce you to the concept of time value of money.

- It explains how time value of money quantifies the value of a dollar today compared to the value of a dollar in the future.

- The chapter will demonstrate why a lawyer needs to understand how to value a future stream of cash flows—say from an annual payout from a divorcing spouse—to be able to advise the client about the settlement offer.

- This chapter will help you learn how to calculate present value and future value, helpful knowledge for advising clients.

- This chapter includes a problem set where you can practice calculating how present value might impact a client's claim for damages.

A. Time Value of Money and Inflation

I will share up front that time value of money is one of those concepts that appears harder than it is. But it is a concept that is oddly intuitive. Before we get into time value of money though, let's start with the related concept of inflation. All of us have stories of our grandparents asking us some innocuous question such as "How much did you pay for gas?" or "How much does it cost to go to the movies?" and receiving some incredulous response that includes something like, "When I was a kid, I was able to mail a letter for ten cents," or "We bought our house for only $50,000," or, a student's personal favorite, "Your tuition is how much?? I worked my way through law school and only paid $600 per year!" Aside from eliciting a deep exhale and a hearty eye roll from you, these conversations also introduced you to the concept of inflation.

Inflation is fundamentally about the buying power of a dollar. It is premised on the concept that a dollar today is worth more than a dollar tomorrow. This concept leads to the fundamental principle that money is worth more the earlier it is received. In other words, the dollar in your pocket today has greater value, and thus greater buying power, than the identical sum in your pocket in the future. Thus, while $600 earned in 1950 could buy you a year's tuition at a law school (seriously, I'm not kidding—look up the footnote[1]), that same $600 today barely covers a year's worth of law school books...yes, yes, as the author of one of those law school books, I do appreciate the irony of this example. Why is there this discrepancy in the buying power of a dollar? After all, it's the exact same dollar bill that was around years ago (if you don't believe me, look at the year of printing on your cash stash). How is it that the exact same dollar bought so much seventy years ago compared to so little now? While the dollar itself hasn't changed, the value of that dollar has. Why is that? Some of that shift is based on other market changes, but mostly the cost of goods and services increase each year because of inflation.

1. Inflation

The United States Federal Reserve ("Federal Reserve") defines inflation as follows:

> ...the increase in the prices of goods and services over time. Inflation cannot be measured by an increase in the cost of one product or service, or even several products or services. Rather, inflation is a general increase in the overall price level of the goods and services in the economy. Federal Reserve policymakers evaluate changes in inflation by monitoring several different price indexes. A price index measures changes in the price of a group of goods and services. The Fed considers several price indexes because different indexes track different products and services, and because indexes are calculated differently. Therefore, various indexes can send diverse signals about inflation.[2]

---

1. https://archives.upenn.edu/exhibits/penn-history/tuition/tuition-1950-1959.
2. https://www.federalreserve.gov/faqs/economy_14419.htm.

The Consumer Price Index ("CPI") is the most widely used indicator of inflation.[3] The United States Bureau of Labor Statistics defines the CPI as "a measure of the average change over time in the prices paid by urban consumers for a market basket of consumer goods and services."[4] To determine the CPI, "the goods and services used to calculate the CPI are collected in 75 urban areas throughout the country and from about 23,000 retail and service establishments."[5]

To recap, inflation, as determined most commonly by the CPI, reflects the increase in the price of goods and services over time. Inflation demonstrates the dollar's value, or purchasing power, given that the prices of goods and services increase over time. So, inflation focuses on the price of goods and services which affects the buying power of a dollar given that, over time, the same goods and services—such as law school tuition—require more dollars to purchase.

Mind you, this is a quick overview of a very complex discipline—Economics. But, as you have read many times now, as lawyers, we primarily only need to have a working familiarity with these concepts, not necessarily an economics degree.

2. Time Value of Money

Time value of money is a concept about quantifying the value of money received today compared to the value of money received at another point in time. For example, if you have $1,000 today, you can invest that money at 5% thus earning $50 and have $1,050 in one year. The difference between the $1,000 today and the $1,050 in a year is the concept of time value of money—the calculable difference between the value of money at two different points in time. When you convert, or in finance parlance "discount," the value of a future stream of cash flows or a future lump sum to today's value, that is calculating present value. When you convert a current stream of cash flows or a current lump sum from today's dollars to a future value, that is calculating future value. Seems pretty straightforward, doesn't it? Well, I am about to complicate it a touch. Here goes—

Using industry parlance, how do you calculate the present value of a future stream of cash flows? In other words, how do you convert the value of cash flows that will be received in the future to a current value in today's dollars?

<u>Cash Inflow Example</u>

Consider this example—if you are like most law students, you (and your parents) are *very* interested in your income post-graduation. So, if you want to earn, let's say $100,000 per year for the first three years after you graduate, you can calculate the lump sum present value of that $100,000 in today's dollars. In this example, you would calculate the present value of that $100,000 income earned after graduation

---

3. https://www.bls.gov/cpi/overview.htm.
4. https://www.bls.gov/cpi/.
5. https://www.bls.gov/cpi/overview.htm.

after three years of law school. That means you are calculating income earned in Year 4, Year 5, and Year 6 since Years 1–3 will be spent toiling away at the joy that is law school. Given that, your calculation would look something like this:

| Lump sum today (present value) | $=$ | present value of $100,000 received in Year 4 | $+$ | present value of $100,000 received in Year 5 | $+$ | present value of $100,000 received in Year 6 |

The formula for which looks like this:

$$\text{Present Value} = \frac{\$100{,}000}{(1+r)^4} + \frac{\$100{,}000}{(1+r)^5} + \frac{\$100{,}000}{(1+r)^6}$$

Now, what is that "r" in our formula you are wondering? Since we are converting the value of money from a future point in time (years four through six) to today's value (which is called the present value), you would need a conversion rate. In finance, when converting a future value of money, whether a stream of cash flows or a lump sum to a present value, that conversion rate is called a "discount rate." The discount rate is simply the conversion rate used to discount a future stream of cash flows or a future lump sum to the present value. That's it! That's the concept of present value. The calculations are decidedly more complicated, but you now have the foundational principal.

The discount rate can be a tricky concept. Choosing which discount rate to use is mostly left to the business consultants, but let's engage in a quick overview here. Choosing the discount rate involves choosing a rate that reflects the cost of that future stream of cash flows. For example, to determine a discount rate for that tantalizing future stream of $100,000 per year upon graduation, let's consider the cost of the money you are using to attend law school. The money you are using to pay your tuition while in law school is not without cost. If you are borrowing money at 6% to pay your tuition, the cost of that loan would be your interest rate which you could use as your discount rate.

The above formula is calculating the present value of a future stream of cash inflows—that all important salary you will earn upon graduation. Let us now consider a different example. Instead of calculating the present value of a future stream of cash inflows, let's determine the present value of a future stream of cash outflows.

Cash Outflow Example

Let's use the example of how much you pay in law school tuition every year and then discount that cash outflow back to today's dollar. Law school tuition is approximately $50,000 per year (oh, stop giving me the side eye, I *know* of course that does not include living expenses). *Assuming* that law school tuition is $50,000 per year, how much would three years of law school tuition be? Intuitively, you will say that it costs $150,000 ($50,000 per year for three years). That is not quite accurate, because as we discussed earlier, the cash you use to pay law school tuition is not without cost. Many law students must borrow the cost of their tuition, so students must pay interest for those loans. If the interest rate for your law school loan is 6%, then that is the discount rate you could use to calculate the present value of your upcoming cash outflows over years one through three of law school. So, your formula to calculate the present value of your future stream of cash outflows would look something like this (the negative in front of each $50,000 indicates that is a cash *outflow*). To my math-phobes out there—take a deep breath, as we are about to play with some formulas:

$$\text{Present Value} = \frac{(-\$50,000)}{(1+6\%)^1} + \frac{(-\$50,000)}{(1+6\%)^2} + \frac{(-\$50,000)}{(1+6\%)^3}$$

Cash Inflow and Cash Outflow Combined Example

Now, here comes the fun part—you can use these formulas to compare (i) the present value of the cost of three-years of law school tuition paid with loans at a 6% interest rate, (ii) with the present value of the income you anticipate earning in the first three years after law school graduation. Such a comparison helps you evaluate whether (i) the present value of your future cash outflows as a result of going to law school are greater than (ii) the present value of your future cash inflows in the first three years after graduation. Admittedly, the cost of going to law school is not only the tuition you pay (there are living expenses as well as the income you forgo by not working). However, this example is not intended to encompass all costs, but is a simple calculation to help demonstrate the concept of time value of money. To compare your cash outflows with your anticipated cash inflows, you would simply combine the formulas as follows:

$$\text{Total} = \frac{(-\$50,000)}{(1+6\%)^1} + \frac{(-\$50,000)}{(1+6\%)^2} + \frac{(-\$50,000)}{(1+6\%)^3} + \frac{(\$100,000)}{(1+8\%)^4} + \frac{(\$100,000)}{(1+8\%)^5} + \frac{(\$100,000)}{(1+8\%)^6}$$

Curious to see what the answer is? Let's calculate it:

$$\text{Total} = \frac{(-\$50{,}000)}{(1.06)^1} + \frac{(-\$50{,}000)}{(1.06)^2} + \frac{(-\$50{,}000)}{(1.06)^3} + \frac{(\$100{,}000)}{(1.08)^4} + \frac{(\$100{,}000)}{(1.08)^5} + \frac{(\$100{,}000)}{(1.08)^6}$$

$$\text{Total} = \frac{(-\$50{,}000)}{1.06} + \frac{(-\$50{,}000)}{1.124} + \frac{(-\$50{,}000)}{1.191} + \frac{(\$100{,}000)}{1.36} + \frac{(\$100{,}000)}{1.469} + \frac{(\$100{,}000)}{1.587}$$

$$\text{Total} = (-\$47{,}170) + (-\$44{,}484) + (-\$41{,}982) + \$73{,}529 + \$68{,}074 + \$63{,}012$$

$$\text{Total} = (-\$133{,}636) + \$204{,}615$$

$$\text{Total} = \$70{,}979$$

(hint: if this number is positive, this is a good thing!)

The terms we used in this section are defined below for those of you who prefer definitions:

- **Present Value** ("PV")—the value of a dollar in today's dollars
- **Future Value** ("FV")—the value of a dollar at some specified future date (in future dollars)
- **Rate** ("r")—the discount rate used to discount future dollars into today's dollars (to discount future value to present value)
- **Number of Periods** ("n")—the period in which the cash inflow or cash outflow occurs

Combining the formulas and the definitions results in this equation:

$$PV = \frac{FV}{(1 + r)^n} \quad \textit{(the sum of the cash inflows and cash outflows calculated for each year)}$$

This formula works for (i) converting a future lump sum of money into a lump sum of money in today's dollars, and (ii) converting a future stream of cash flows to a lump sum of money in today's dollars. To use the proper lingo, this formula allows you to (i) discount a future value lump sum to a present value lump sum, and (ii) calculate the present value of a future stream of cash flows. If you want to see that formula for the present value for a future stream of cash flows, it is the same formula but written like this:

$$PV = \frac{CF}{(1+r)^t} + \frac{CF}{(1+r)^t} + \cdots \frac{CF}{(1+r)^n}$$

Where:

- **Present Value** ("PV")—the value of a dollar in today's dollars
- **Cash Flow** ("CF")—a future stream of cash flows. This means a stream of periodic, regular or irregular, cash payments that will be received in the future (kind of like the stream of salary payments you all frequently tell me that you eagerly await upon graduation)
- **Rate** ("r")—the discount rate used to discount future dollars into today's dollars (to discount future value to present value)
- **Time Periods** ("t") and ("n")—the time period in which you are expecting to receive the stream of cash flows and "n" is the time period in which you are expecting to receive the final cash flow

As you can see, the present value of multiple cash flows to be received in the future is simply the sum of the present value of those multiple cash flows.

B. Annuity

Another type of future stream of cash flows is called an "Annuity." While annuity has many different meanings depending on whether we are considering life insurance or finance, here, an annuity is simply a fixed sum of money received over a fixed period of time.

C. Time Value of Money in Law Practice

Legal Highlights

Time Value of Money

Alright! Now that we have reviewed the basics, as you can see, the formulas for calculating a lump calculation and a stream of cash flows look similar. Why, oh why am I asking you to learn this, you may wonder? Well, I'm glad you asked! Imagine the following:

Family Law. You are a family law lawyer, and you have a client who is amicably divorcing from her wife. Client is seeking alimony, and Client's soon to be ex-wife is offering to pay either (i) $250,000 in a lump sum payment at the close of negotiations or, (ii) $50,000 every year for the next five years. Your client, perplexed, looks at you confused and says, "isn't that the same thing?" As a family law attorney with an understanding of the time value of money, you can explain to your client that these amounts are not the same and also to negotiate with opposing counsel on a sufficient settlement.

Personal Injury Law. You are a personal injury lawyer representing five clients who were all injured because of a faulty ignitor switch in their car. The clients tell you that they need to be compensated for their injuries, especially since they will not be able to work at all for the next three years during their recovery. The automobile manufacturer offers a lump sum settlement for each of your clients. How do you calculate whether that lump sum financially compensates your clients sufficiently for their loss of future salary payments?

Wills, Trusts and Estates Law. A client calls you and tells you that he has won the Georgia State Lottery ("Lottery")! He calls you requesting your help in devising his estate. He says that the Lottery is asking him whether he wants the cash option or the annuity option. You pull up the Lottery website to read their rules and regulations (because as a good lawyer, you remember your legal research and writing professor impressing upon you that Wikipedia is not sufficient legal research, so going to the source of the law, rule or regulation is best. Sorry, law professor mini rant here). Here is an excerpt from the Georgia Lottery Powerball Rules and Regulations:

> "30.1(a) Grand Prizes shall be paid, at the election of the player made no later than sixty (60) days after the player becomes entitled to the prize, with either a per-winner annuity or single lump sum payment (which may be referred to as the "cash option"). If the payment election is not made at the time of purchase and is not made by the player within sixty (60) days after the player becomes entitled to the prize, then the prize shall be paid as an annuity prize. An election for an annuity payment made by a player before ticket purchase or by system default or design

may be changed to a cash option payment at the election of the player until the expiration of sixty (60) days after the player becomes entitled to the prize. The election to take the cash option payment may be made at the time of the prize claim or within sixty (60) days after the player becomes entitled to the prize. An election made after the winner becomes entitled to the prize is final and cannot be revoked, withdrawn, or otherwise changed. (https://www.galottery.com/content/dam/portal /pdfs/player-zone/powerball-official-game-rules.pdf)

"30.1 (b) ... Winner(s) who elect a cash option payment shall be paid their share(s) in a single lump sum payment (https://www.galottery.com /content/dam/portal/pdfs/player-zone/powerball-official-game-rules .pdf)

"30.1 (e) All annuitized prizes shall be paid annually in thirty (30) payments with the initial payment being made in a single payment, to be followed by twenty-nine (29) payments funded by the annuity. Except as may be controlled by a Selling Lottery's governing statute, all annuitized prizes shall be paid annually in thirty (30) graduated payments (increasing each year) by a rate as determined by the Product Group. Prize payments may be rounded down to the nearest one thousand dollars ($1,000.00). Annual payments after the initial payment shall be made by the lottery on the anniversary date or if such date falls on a non-business day, then the first business day following the anniversary date of the selection of the Grand Prize-Winning Numbers." (https:// www.galottery.com/content/dam/portal/pdfs/player-zone/powerball -official-game-rules.pdf)

Now, let's apply what you have learned about time value of money in the following case study.

D. Chapter 6 Time Value of Money Exercises and Case Studies

Case Study 6.1—Time Value of Money

You are a trial lawyer representing a man ("Client") who worked for a coal shipping company ("Company") in Pennsylvania. Client tells you that on January 13, 1978, he was carrying a piece of heavy equipment on Company's barge which had patches of ice and snow. He tells you that he slipped and fell, landing on his tailbone, and the piece of heavy equipment then fell in his lap. Client tells you that the injury made him permanently unable to return to his job. However, a year and a half later after seeing several doctors, he was cleared to perform light work only as of July 1, 1979, but could not return to working as previously employed. Client comes to you seeking your assistance in suing his employer for damages. Client states that he planned to retire at age 65 on June 27, 1990.

You summarize the information from Client as follows:

Annual Salary at the time of the accident: $26,025

Date of Accident: Jan 13, 1978

Date Available for Light Work: July 1, 1979

Anticipated Date of Retirement: June 27, 1990
(12.5 years from Date of Accident to Anticipated Date of Retirement)

Pain and Suffering Request: $50,000

Medical Bills: N/A—paid by insurance company

Questions for Case Study 6.1

1. Assuming that the doctrine of negligence holds valid in this case, and you want your Client to be appropriately compensated for his losses directly stemming from his injury, list the items for which you would sue.

2. Calculate the amount you would claim in damages for Client.

<u>Your Potential Initial Request</u>

Your answer may have looked something like $375,312.50, calculated as follows:

Damages for Salary: $325,312.50
(= $26,025 of annual salary x 12.5 which is the number of years working)

Damages for Pain and Suffering: $50,000

Total Damages: $375,312.50
(= $325,312.50 + $50,000 payment for pain and suffering)

<u>Potential Opposing Counsel Response</u>

After you calculate the amount you would claim for damages for Client, you send your findings to the opposing counsel representing the company.

Opposing counsel responds that settlement should be no more than $275,881.50 calculated as follows:

Annual Salary at the time of the accident:	$26,025
Projected Earnings from date of injury until the expected date of retirement:	$325,312.50[6] ($26,025 of annual salary x 12.5 which is the number of years of working = $325,312.50)
Pain and Suffering:	$50,000
Projected Earnings from Light Work:	$66,352[7]
Previous payments from Company to Client:	$33,079[8]
Medical Bills:	N/A—paid by insurance company

$325,312.50 + $50,000 – $66,352 – $33,079 = $275,881.50

Continuation of Questions for Case Study 6.1

3. Review the above. Would $275,881.50 be the amount for which you would settle? Is anything missing? No, no, not intending to hide the ball here as we professors know how much you students *love* that. But, to help you understand the analysis and the different arguments, take a moment, step back from the reading, think about what we have discussed in this Chapter and determine whether you think something is missing from the analysis.

Potential Adjustments to Damages Claims

Ok, to help you think about what is missing, think about Client's salary. At the time of the accident, Client earned $26,025 and planned to work for another 12.5 years. Would Client earn the exact same salary every year for 12.5 years? As Client's counsel, could you argue that Client's salary would likely increase over that period of time? What are some of the reasons Client's salary could increase over time? Here are some possibilities:

---

6. Client is injured on Jan 13, 1978, and retiring on Jun 27, 1990, thus Client had a work expectancy of 12.5 years. Multiply Client's annual salary at the time of the accident of $26,025 by the 12.5 work expectancy to arrive at $325,312.50 as the amount of Client's projected earnings from the date of injury until the expected date of retirement.

7. Remember, Client was cleared to do light work as of July 1, 1979. So, from that date until the expected date of retirement, Client can earn at least minimum wage being employed to do light work. Opposing counsel is arguing that Company should not be required to compensate Client's total salary, but instead Company should only be required to compensate Client for Client's Projected Earnings from date of injury until the expected date of retirement *less* what Client can earn by working a job paying minimum wage during that time period.

8. Company continued to pay Client a salary after the date of the accident, thus, Company is arguing that while Client was entitled to earn Client's salary from the date of the accident until Client's anticipated retirement date, Company should deduct not only what Client can earn from a minimum wage job but also deduct any salary payments Company paid to Client after the date of the accident.

i. *Promotions*

- Client, if a qualified employee, might earn promotions over that period of time earning him a higher salary.

ii. *Bonuses*

- Client may have been eligible for bonuses.

iii. *Union Negotiated Wage Increases*

- If Client is a member of a union, it is not unusual for union contracts to mandate annual percentage wage increases for its members. Such a provision, were it applicable to Client, would increase Client's annual salary over time.

iv. *Inflation*

- As you now know from this chapter's readings, inflation makes a dollar worth more today than that same dollar would be worth tomorrow. Thus, if a dollar today is worth more than a dollar tomorrow, Client's $26,025 annual salary will have diminishing buying power every succeeding year. In other words, the $26,025 salary this year will be worth less year after year. Thus, if Client is receiving his future $26,025 yearly salary in a lump sum payment today, that lump sum would not be the equivalent of $26,025 multiplied by 12.5 years.

If you requested any of the above, the lump sum of money for which you would sue on Client's behalf would be greater than the $275,881.50 calculated so far. In response to opposing counsel's arguments, you send over your request with a note that the any damages settlement should be adjusted for Items (i)–(iv) above.

Before moving on, take a moment and anticipate what opposing counsel's arguments might be in response. As an attorney, you should always prepare for opposing counsel's arguments. Articulating what you anticipate opposing counsel's arguments will be will help you craft arguments that can withstand opposing counsel's response.

Potential Opposing Counsel's 2nd Response

Ok! Company's lawyers view your proposed adjustments for damages and counter with the following:

i. *Promotions*
   a. **Speculative.** Company rejects adjustments to damages for projected earnings from anticipated promotions arguing that client may not have received many merit increases because he may have had performance issues that would have suppressed any promotions.

ii. *Bonuses*
   a. **Speculative.** Company rejects including bonuses in the calculation of damages for salary because bonuses are not guaranteed, and it is

impossible to project how much a bonus would be or whether a bonus would be offered at all.

   iii. *Union Negotiated Wage Increases*
       a. **Possible.** Needs to be verified by reviewing the union contract and whether Client is eligible for the wage increases.

   iv. *Inflation*
       a. **Inflation will be Low.** Company rejects that there would be an annual cost of living adjustment given that, at the time of the accident, inflation was very low. Additionally, Company argues that projecting inflation is highly speculative and thus should be excluded from the analysis.

   v. *Investment Return*
       a. Company introduces a new argument that Client's investment earnings from the settlement award should be considered when calculating damages. According to Company, since Client will receive a lump sum for the settlement, Client will likely invest that lump sum and thus earn a return. Company argues that the goal of the settlement is to provide Client with the earnings that Client would have received absent Client's injury. Thus, any investment earnings from the settlement award should not provide Client a surplus but should reduce the total settlement award so that the settlement award plus the investment return approximates Client's anticipated projected earnings.

Case study 6.1 is a simplified version of the types of analysis you would do as an attorney, and it gives you some idea of where the sticking points are in these types of analysis. While your law firm will likely have a business consultant on hand to complete the actual calculations, you, as the attorney, will negotiate the items to include in the calculation, draft the brief for the court, and negotiate these issues with opposing counsel. It is vital for you to understand how these items will impact your client's total damage award for you to be an effective advocate for your client.

Now that you understand the broad strokes of time value of money, read the following Supreme Court case (the facts will be familiar to you!) to reinforce your newfound knowledge. Recognize that different courts and different lawyers will take different approaches in determining whether inflation and potential wage increases should be taken into consideration when calculating lost wages. This case should give you an understanding of what is included and excluded and the corresponding rationale. As you read this case, focus on the court's reasonings for why wage increases might happen (individual and societal reasons) and a court's interest in using calculation methods that balance predictability and simplicity with accuracy.

Jones & Laughlin Steel Corp. v. Pfeifer

462 U.S. 523
Supreme Court of the United States
February 28, 1983, Argued; June 15, 1983, Decided

JUSTICE STEVENS delivered the opinion of the Court.

Respondent was injured in the course of his employment as a loading helper on a coal barge. As his employer, petitioner was required to compensate him for his injury under § 4 of the Longshoremen's and Harbor Workers' Compensation Act (Act). 44 Stat. 1426, 33 U.S.C. § 904…. We granted certiorari to…consider whether the Court of Appeals correctly upheld the trial court's computation of respondent's damages….

Petitioner owns a fleet of barges that it regularly operates on three navigable rivers in the vicinity of Pittsburgh, Pa. Respondent was employed for 19 years to aid in loading and unloading those barges at one of petitioner's plants located on the shore of the Monongahela River. On January 13, 1978, while carrying a heavy pump, respondent slipped and fell on snow and ice that petitioner had negligently failed to remove from the gunnels of a barge. His injury made him permanently unable to return to his job with the petitioner, or to perform anything other than light work after July 1, 1979.

In November 1979, respondent brought this action against petitioner, alleging that his injury had been "caused by the negligence of the vessel" within the meaning of § 5(b) of the Act. The District Court found in favor of respondent and awarded damages of $275,881.36….

The District Court's calculation of damages was predicated on a few undisputed facts. At the time of his injury respondent was earning an annual wage of $26,025. He had a remaining work expectancy of 12 ½ years. On the date of trial (October 1, 1980), respondent had received compensation payments of $33,079.14. If he had obtained light work and earned the legal minimum hourly wage from July 1, 1979, until his 65th birthday, he would have earned $66,352.

The District Court arrived at its final award by taking 12 ½ years of earnings at respondent's wage at the time of injury ($325,312.50), subtracting his projected hypothetical earnings at the minimum wage ($66,352) and the compensation payments he had received under § 4 ($33,079.14), and adding $50,000 for pain and suffering. The court did not increase the award to take inflation into account, and it did not discount the award to reflect the present value of the future stream of income….

… The Court of Appeals next held that in defining the content of that law, inflation must be taken into account:

"Full compensation for lost prospective earnings is most difficult, if not impossible, to attain if the court is blind to the realities of the consumer price index and the recent historical decline of purchasing power. Thus if we recognize, as we must, that the injured worker is entitled to reimbursement for his loss of future earnings, an honest and accurate calculation must consider the stark reality of inflationary conditions.[1] ...

The Damages Issue

The District Court found that respondent was permanently disabled as a result of petitioner's negligence. He therefore was entitled to an award of damages to compensate him for his probable pecuniary loss over the duration of his career, reduced to its present value. It is useful at the outset to review the way in which damages should be measured in a hypothetical inflation-free economy. We shall then consider how price inflation alters the analysis....

I

In calculating damages, it is assumed that if the injured party had not been disabled, he would have continued to work, and to receive wages at periodic intervals until retirement, disability, or death. An award for impaired earning capacity is intended to compensate the worker for the diminution in that stream of income.[8] The award could in theory take the form of periodic payments, but in this country it has traditionally taken the form of a lump sum, paid at the conclusion of the litigation.[9] The appropriate lump sum cannot be computed without first examining the stream of income it purports to replace.

The lost stream's length cannot be known with certainty; the worker could have been disabled or even killed in a different, non-work-related accident at any time. The probability that he would still be working at a given date is constantly diminishing.[10] Given the complexity of trying to make an exact calculation, litigants frequently follow the relatively simple course of assuming that the worker would have continued to work up until a specific date certain. In this case, for example, both parties agreed that the petitioner would have continued to work until age 65 (12 ½ more years) if he had not been injured.

---

1. [Omitted]

8. See generally D. Dobbs, Law of Remedies § 8.1 (1973). It should be noted that in a personal injury action such as this one, damages for impaired earning capacity are awarded to compensate the injured person for his loss. In a wrongful-death action, a similar but not identical item of damages is awarded for the manner in which diminished earning capacity harms either the worker's survivors or his estate. See generally 1 S. Speiser, Recovery for Wrongful Death 2d, ch. 3 (1975) (hereafter Speiser). Since the problem of incorporating inflation into the award is the same in both types of action, we shall make occasional reference to wrongful-death actions in this opinion.

9. [Omitted]

10. [Omitted]

Each annual installment[11] in the lost stream comprises several elements. The most significant is, of course, the actual wage. In addition, the worker may have enjoyed certain fringe benefits, which should be included in an ideal evaluation of the worker's loss but are frequently excluded for simplicity's sake.[12] On the other hand, the injured worker's lost wages would have been diminished by state and federal income taxes. Since the damages award is tax-free, the relevant stream is ideally of after-tax wages and benefits. See *Norfolk & Western R. Co. v. Liepelt*, 444 U.S. 490 (1980). Moreover, workers often incur unreimbursed costs, such as transportation to work and uniforms, that the injured worker will not incur. These costs should also be deducted in estimating the lost stream.

In this case the parties appear to have agreed to simplify the litigation, and to presume that in each installment all the elements in the stream would offset each other, except for gross wages. However, in attempting to estimate even such a stylized stream of annual installments of gross wages, a trier of fact faces a complex task. The most obvious and most appropriate place to begin is with the worker's annual wage at the time of injury. Yet the "estimate of the loss from lessened earnings capacity in the future need not be based solely upon the wages which the plaintiff was earning at the time of his injury." C. McCormick, Damages § 86, p. 300 (1935). Even in an inflation-free economy—that is to say one in which the prices of consumer goods remain stable—a worker's wages tend to "inflate." This "real" wage inflation reflects a number of factors, some linked to the specific individual and some linked to broader societal forces.[13]

With the passage of time, an individual worker often becomes more valuable to his employer. His personal work experiences increase his hourly contributions to firm profits. To reflect that heightened value, he will often receive "seniority" or "experience" raises, "merit" raises, or even promotions.[14] Although it may be difficult to prove when, and whether, a particular injured worker might have received such wage increases....

Furthermore, the wages of workers as a class may increase over time. See *Grunenthal v. Long Island R. Co.*, 393 U.S. 156, 160 (1968). Through more efficient interaction among labor, capital, and technology, industrial productivity may increase, and

---

11. Obviously, another distorting simplification is being made here. Although workers generally receive their wages in weekly or biweekly installments, virtually all calculations of lost earnings, including the one made in this case, pretend that the stream would have flowed in large spurts, taking the form of annual installments.

12. These might include insurance coverage, pension and retirement plans, profit sharing, and in-kind services....

13. As will become apparent, in speaking of "societal" forces we are primarily concerned with those macroeconomic forces that influence wages in the worker's particular industry. The term will be used to encompass all forces that tend to inflate a worker's wage without regard to the worker's individual characteristics.

14. It is also possible that a worker could be expected to change occupations completely. See, *e.g.*, *Stearns Coal & Lumber Co. v. Williams*, 164 Ky. 618, 176 S. W. 15 (1915).

workers' wages may enjoy a share of that growth.[16] Such productivity increases—reflected in real increases in the gross national product per worker-hour—have been a permanent feature of the national economy since the conclusion of World War II.[17] Moreover, through collective bargaining, workers may be able to negotiate increases in their "share" of revenues…. Either of these forces could affect the lost stream of income in an inflation-free economy. In this case, the plaintiff's proffered evidence on predictable wage growth may have reflected the influence of either or both of these two factors.

To summarize, the first stage in calculating an appropriate award for lost earnings involves an estimate of what the lost stream of income would have been. The stream may be approximated as a series of after-tax payments, one in each year of the worker's expected remaining career. In estimating what those payments would have been in an inflation-free economy, the trier of fact may begin with the worker's annual wage at the time of injury. If sufficient proof is offered, the trier of fact may increase that figure to reflect the appropriate influence of individualized factors (such as foreseeable promotions) and societal factors (such as foreseeable productivity growth within the worker's industry).[19]

Of course, even in an inflation-free economy the award of damages to replace the lost stream of income cannot be computed simply by totaling up the sum of the periodic payments. For the damages award is paid in a lump sum at the conclusion of the litigation, and when it—or even a part of it—is invested, it will earn additional money. It has been settled since our decision in *Chesapeake & Ohio R. Co. v. Kelly*, 241 U.S. 485 (1916), that "in all cases where it is reasonable to suppose that interest may safely be earned upon the amount that is awarded, the ascertained future benefits ought to be discounted in the making up of the award." *Id.*, at 490.[20]

The discount rate should be based on the rate of interest that would be earned on "the best and safest investments." Id., at 491. Once it is assumed that the injured worker would definitely have worked for a specific term of years, he is entitled to a risk-free stream of future income to replace his lost wages; therefore, the discount rate should not reflect the market's premium for investors who are willing to accept some risk of default….

Thus, although the notion of a damages award representing the present value of a lost stream of earnings in an inflation-free economy rests on some fairly sophisticated economic concepts, the two elements that determine its calculation can be

---

16. P. Samuelson, Economics 738–756 (10th ed. 1976) (hereafter Samuelson).

17. [Omitted]

19. If foreseeable real wage growth is shown, it may produce a steadily increasing series of payments, with the first payment showing the least increase from the wage at the time of injury and the last payment showing the most.

20. Although this rule could be seen as a way of ensuring that the lump-sum award accurately represents the pecuniary injury as of the time of trial, it was explained by reference to the duty to mitigate damages. 241 U.S., at 489–490.

stated fairly easily. They are: (1) the amount that the employee would have earned during each year that he could have been expected to work after the injury; and (2) the appropriate discount rate, reflecting the safest available investment. The trier of fact should apply the discount rate to each of the estimated installments in the lost stream of income, and then add up the discounted installments to determine the total award.[22]

II

Unfortunately for triers of fact, ours is not an inflation-free economy. Inflation has been a permanent fixture in our economy for many decades, and there can be no doubt that it ideally should affect both stages of the calculation described in the previous section. The difficult problem is how it can do so in the practical context of civil litigation under § 5(b) of the Act.

The first stage of the calculation required an estimate of the shape of the lost stream of future income. For many workers, including respondent, a contractual "cost-of-living adjustment" automatically increases wages each year by the percentage change during the previous year in the consumer price index calculated by the Bureau of Labor Statistics. Such a contract provides a basis for taking into account an additional societal factor—price inflation—in estimating the worker's lost future earnings.

The second stage of the calculation requires the selection of an appropriate discount rate. Price inflation—or more precisely, anticipated price inflation—certainly affects market rates of return. If a lender knows that his loan is to be repaid a year later with dollars that are less valuable than those he has advanced, he will charge an interest rate that is high enough both to compensate him for the temporary use of the loan proceeds and also to make up for their shrinkage in value.[23]...

---

22. At one time it was thought appropriate to distinguish between compensating a plaintiff "for the loss of time from his work which has actually occurred up to the time of trial" and compensating him "for the time which he will lose in [the] future." C. McCormick, Damages § 86 (1935). This suggested that estimated future earning capacity should be discounted to the date of trial, and a separate calculation should be performed for the estimated loss of earnings between injury and trial. *Id.*, §§ 86, 87. It is both easier and more precise to discount the entire lost stream of earnings back to the date of injury—the moment from which earning capacity was impaired. The plaintiff may then be awarded interest on that discounted sum for the period between injury and judgment, in order to ensure that the award when invested will still be able to replicate the lost stream. See *In re Air Crash Disaster Near Chicago, Illinois, on May 25, 1979*, 644 F.2d 633, 641–646 (CA7 1981); 1 Speiser § 8:6, p. 723.

23. The effect of price inflation on the discount rate may be less speculative than its effect on the lost stream of future income. The latter effect always requires a prediction of the future, for the existence of a contractual cost-of-living adjustment gives no guidance about how big that adjustment will be in some future year. However, whether the discount rate also turns on predictions of the future depends on how it is assumed that the worker will invest his award.

On the one hand, it might be assumed that at the time of the award the worker will invest in a mixture of safe short-term, medium-term, and long-term bonds, with one scheduled to mature each year of his expected worklife. In that event, by purchasing bonds immediately after judgment, the

... For our review of the foregoing cases leads us to draw three conclusions. First, by its very nature the calculation of an award for lost earnings must be a rough approximation. Because the lost stream can never be predicted with complete confidence, any lump sum represents only a "rough and ready" effort to put the plaintiff in the position he would have been in had he not been injured. Second, sustained price inflation can make the award substantially less precise. Inflation's current magnitude and unpredictability create a substantial risk that the damages award will prove to have little relation to the lost wages it purports to replace. Third, the question of lost earnings can arise in many different contexts. In some sectors of the economy, it is far easier to assemble evidence of an individual's most likely career path than in others....

III

... On remand, the decision on whether to reopen the record should be left to the sound discretion of the trial court. It bears mention that the present record already gives reason to believe a fair award may be more confidently expected in this case than in many. The employment practices in the longshoring industry appear relatively stable and predictable. The parties seem to have had no difficulty in arriving at the period of respondent's future work expectancy, or in predicting the character of the work that he would have been performing during that entire period if he had not been injured. Moreover, the record discloses that respondent's wages were determined by a collective-bargaining agreement that explicitly provided for "cost of living" increases, *id.*, at 310, and that recent company history also included a "general" increase and a "job class increment increase." ...

IV

... The judgment of the Court of Appeals is vacated, and the case is remanded for further proceedings consistent with this opinion.

It is so ordered.

———————————

As you can see, a court considers factors when determining an award—inflation, cost of living wage increases, merit bonuses, and investment earnings, just to name a few. This case should give you a better understanding of time value of money and how it finds its way into legal analysis.

———————————

worker can be ensured whatever future stream of nominal income is predicted. Since all relevant effects of inflation on the market interest rate will have occurred at that time, future changes in the rate of price inflation will have no effect on the stream of income he receives.... On the other hand, it might be assumed that the worker will invest exclusively in safe short-term notes, reinvesting them at the new market rate whenever they mature. Future market rates would be quite important to such a worker. Predictions of what they will be would therefore also be relevant to the choice of an appropriate discount rate, in much the same way that they are always relevant to the first stage of the calculation....

Chapter 6 Highlights

- A dollar today has more buying power than a dollar tomorrow.
- When doing calculations for damages, remember to adjust for future increases in earnings and the impact of inflation.
- The calculation of present value is determining how much to pay today for a future stream of cash flows.

Seven

Capital

- This chapter will teach you the basics of capital acquisition and capital's impact on a client's legal risks.
- The chapter will provide you an overview of the two forms of capital—debt and equity.

A. Capital Overview

Each corporation will need funding, known as capital, to fund and operate its business. It is important to understand that a corporation's ability to operate is dependent on the corporation's ability to generate or obtain capital. Fundamentally, capital is simply cash. A corporation will need capital to pay its operating expenses, such as paying employees, paying utilities, paying income taxes, paying lawyers (!) and leasing or purchasing a location for the corporation to operate. Corporations also need capital to purchase inventory for sale in the company's day to day operations. So, capital—meaning access to cash and cash flow—is vital to a corporation's operations.

Since corporations need capital to operate, corporations need to understand where they can access that capital. Attorneys need to understand how businesses obtain, use and disburse that capital to be able to provide legal guidance on the legal risks of soliciting, obtaining and dispersing that capital.

B. Accessing Capital

Corporations can access capital either from internal sources or external sources:

- To access capital from internal sources, corporations can access capital from cash it already has in its existing cash account, or a corporation can access capital by generating cash from the sale of the corporation's inventory in the corporation's day-to-day operations.

- To access capital from external sources, corporations can access capital by either issuing debt (borrowing money) or issuing equity (selling stock in exchange for money).

Thus, a corporation's need for capital can be satisfied from (i) the corporations's existing cash stash, (ii) earning cash from selling the corporations's inventory, (iii) borrowing cash from third parties, or (iv) selling stock to obtain cash from investors.

Let's review the chart below for a further breakdown:

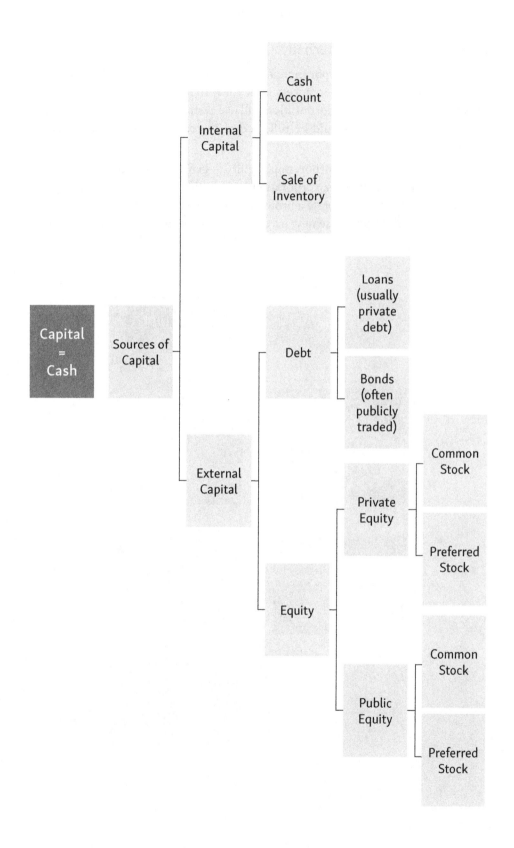

1. Accessing Capital Internally

To understand how a corporation accesses capital internally, first we will start with a corporation's ability to access cash from the corporation's cash account. This simply means that the corporation will use cash that the corporation already has on hand. This cash would be reflected in the cash account on the Balance Sheet.

Now, let us move to the corporation's ability to generate cash from the corporation's sale of inventory. If the corporation is operating productively, the corporation will sell inventory, generate a profit and also generate a positive net cash flow sufficient enough to purchase new inventory and continue the operating cycle as follows:

Company sells inventory for cash OR accounts receivable

Cash from selling inventory is added to the company's cash balance and, thus, the cash balance on the Balance Sheet increases

Company uses the converted cash to acquire more inventory

If the company sells inventory for accounts receivable, company converts the accounts receivable to cash (collects the debt)

2. Accessing Capital Externally

To understand how a corporation accesses capital from external sources, we must first understand why a corporation would seek external sources instead of using only internal sources. Sometimes, the corporation's cash balance is insufficient to satisfy the corporation's capital needs. Additionally, the corporation's inventory sales might also be insufficient to generate the capital the corporation needs. Thus, the corporation might then seek additional capital from an external source. Why would sales of a corporation's inventory generate insufficient cash flow, you might wonder? Well, consider the Income Statement: as you might recall, at the end of a fiscal period, a corporation will have either a net profit or a net loss:

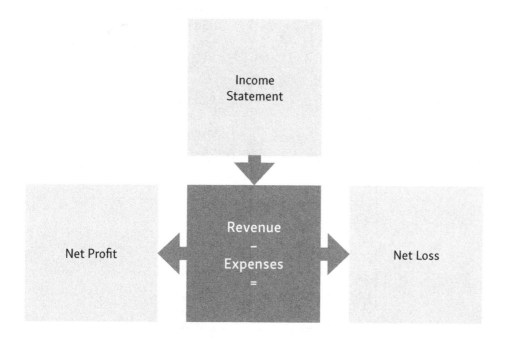

If the corporation has a net profit and a net positive cash flow, what does the corporation do with that net profit? The corporation can either (i) return the profits to shareholders by declaring dividends or by repurchasing shares from shareholders, or (ii) retain the profits in the corporation. If the corporation retains the profits, the corporation can use those retained profits for many purposes including purchasing new inventory, investing in research and development, increasing executive pay, increasing employee compensation or simply to increase the corporation's cash balance. Graphically, you can think of it like this:

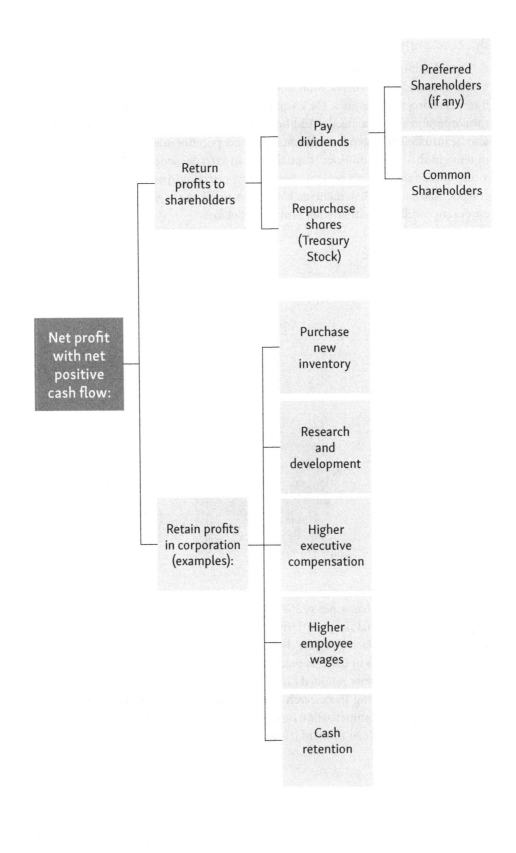

Alternatively, the corporation could have a net loss. For example, a net loss would look as follows:

Income Statement for the period ending December 31, 2018 (in dollars)

Revenue	$10,000,000
Less: Cost of Goods Sold	$2,000,000
= Gross Profit	$8,000,000
Less: Operating Expenses	$8,250,000
= Operating Income	($250,000)
Less: Tax and Interest Expense	$750,000
= Net Loss	($1,000,000)

You might recall that net profit does not automatically mean a positive net cash flow. Similarly, if a corporation has a net loss, that does not necessarily mean that the corporation has a net *cash* loss. However, if a corporation does have a net loss *and* a negative net cash flow, the corporation might require access to external sources of capital as shown below:

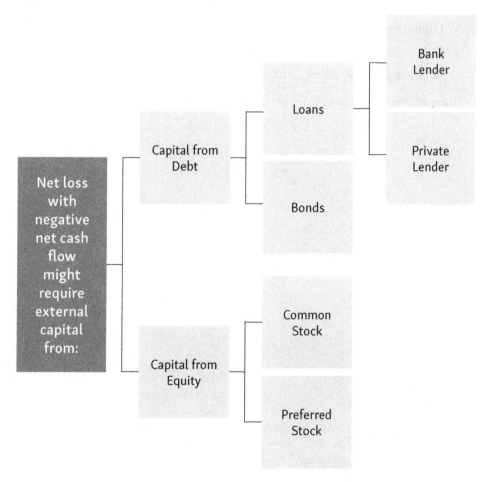

Legal Highlights

Capital

If you have a corporate client that seeks capital from the capital markets, lawyers can have varying responsibilities. Lawyers can be asked to draft or review loan agreements, draft a prospectus for a bond or stock offering, or advise on the laws of securities regulations to determine compliance with securities laws.

Chapter 7 Highlights

- Capital is simply cash, obtained through some combination of equity and debt.
- Capital can be obtained from internal sources or external sources.
- Debt is generally either loans or bonds.
- Equity is generally either common stock or preferred stock.

The next two chapters will discuss debt and equity in more detail.

Eight

Debt Analysis

- This chapter will detail debt as a legally binding contract, the breach of which causes significant legal risks for a lawyer's client and will teach you the basics of debt to help you mitigate your client's legal risks.

- This chapter will also review the basics of debt to help you identify legal risks when drafting, editing, or negotiating the contracts creating debt.

- This chapter includes a case study using a sample prospectus of a debt offering.

A. What Is Debt?

As we learned in the previous chapter, there are two types of capital—debt and equity. This chapter will focus on debt. Debt is a legally binding contract—a loan agreement—between parties where one party (the borrower), agrees to borrow a specified amount of money (the principal) from another party (the lender), who agrees to lend the principal to the borrower. The borrower agrees to repay the principal pursuant to the terms and conditions set forth in the loan agreement.

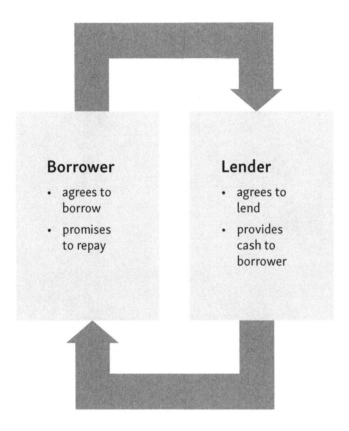

Borrower
- agrees to borrow
- promises to repay

Lender
- agrees to lend
- provides cash to borrower

Let's engage in a thought exercise to think through what those terms and conditions would be. From your first year in law school, you *should* remember that contracts must have sufficient clarity on the rights and obligations of each party to enable a third party to enforce the contract. To determine what that minimum clarity would be for a loan agreement, think about this defensively as an attorney. Say, for example, an attorney notified your client of the attorney's intent to sue your client for breach of a loan agreement. Where would you start and what questions would you want answered before you respond to opposing counsel? You would want to determine questions such as:

1. Is this a legally binding contract?

   - Is your client a named party to the loan agreement?

   - Is this an obligation of your client?

2. Is your client in breach?

   - Is your client liable for the amount claimed by opposing counsel?

   - Did your client have this monetary obligation?

   - If so, did your client breach that monetary obligation?

3. What are the monetary obligations in the performance section of the loan agreement?

   - How much did your client agree to repay in the loan agreement?

   - What are the loan agreement's terms governing the payment date of the debt?

4. What are the loan agreement's terms regarding remedies for nonpayment of the debt?

When you think about these questions in the context of a contract, you realize that you have identified the common terms that you will see in a loan agreement. So, let us consider these terms one at a time.

1. Terms of Debt

   - Parties

     The parties to the loan agreement include, at a minimum, the borrower and the lender. With debt, you have one party who is borrowing money and one party who is lending money. The party who is borrowing money is the borrower, and the party who is lending money is the lender. In essence, the borrower needs capital and decides to seek capital from an external source, the lender. The lender is someone who has excess capital and offers that capital to the borrower with the expectation of repayment.

     Now, the next question becomes, how much is the borrower agreeing to borrow and how much is the lender agreeing to lend? And, what are the terms of the loan?

   - Principal—the amount of money that the borrower borrows from the lender and agrees to repay by the date set forth in the loan agreement.

   - Interest—the amount of money that the lender charges the borrower as a cost of lending the principal.

- Interest Rate—the calculation of how much interest must be repaid. The loan agreement will state the percentage of the principal or a lump sum that the borrower must pay to the lender as interest.
- Maturity Date—the date by when the borrower must repay the debt (principal, interest and any damages) in full to the lender.

As you can see, from an attorney's perspective, debt is simply a contract with terms detailing that contract. Those terms determine how much one party is lending and the other party is borrowing, how much the parties agree will be repaid, when this repayment must occur and any remedies for nonperformance.

As future lawyers, you can think through and visualize the legal process and consequences of a borrower's use of debt:

1. Execution

1. Two parties execute a loan agreement.
2. With that execution, the parties are now legally bound by the terms of the loan agreement.

2. Performance

3. Borrower is required to repay the debt in accordance with the repayment terms of the loan agreement. Those terms often, though not always, require monthly or quarterly repayments of principal and interest.
4. Lender is required to lend the principal in accordance with the loan terms.

3. Breach

5. If borrower misses a payment on the debt as set forth in the loan agreement, borrower is now in breach.
6. The non-breaching party, in this case the lender, often has a contractual obligation to notify the breaching party of the breach. Here, lender, as the non-breaching party, would notify the borrower of the breach.

4. Cure

7. Often, contracts provide the breaching party the right to cure the breach after receiving notification of the breach.
8. The borrower would typically have a cure period—meaning the period of time that the borrower has to cure the breach.

5. Remedies

> 9. If the breach is not cured—meaning if the borrower does not become current on the debt payments owed—the non-breaching party (here, the lender) has the right to enforce the loan agreement, including seeking any monetary and/or equitable damages.

As you can see, a loan agreement (the document memorializing the loan) is simply a legal contract. It is the contract law that you learned about—and, I'm sure just *loved*—from 1L year. This section focuses on the breach of a borrower, which is the more common breaching party to a loan agreement. However, lenders have performance obligations that can also be breached as well.

B. Types of Debt

While there are many forms of debt in finance, the two common categories of debt are loans and bonds. Corporations sometimes need capital and will borrow money to have sufficient cash for the corporation's needs. Bonds and loans are types of debt, and debt is a form of capital. Loans are the most common form of debt used by corporations, consumers and government entities, and bonds are issued by corporations and government entities.

Loans, for law students, are more intuitive as many law students have student loans (yes, yes, I know student loans are a sore subject and I respect that, but I use them as an example because your familiarity with student loans makes it easier for you to visualize this concept). From your experience with student loans, you recognize that you have agreed to borrow a specified amount of money (principal) to be repaid by a future agreed upon date (maturity date) for an agreed upon amount of interest as determined by an interest rate. Loans typically, though not always, are repaid in installments of principal and interest. You likely also know by now that your student loans, like all debt, are legally binding contracts between you and your student loan lenders.

Bonds are a little less intuitive. Like with a loan, corporations need capital and will seek that capital from external sources. However, sometimes the amount a corporation needs to borrow is so large that the corporation seeks that debt from multiple parties. The corporation could seek to borrow, for example, $100 million. Instead of obtaining that amount from 1–2 lenders in a loan, the corporation will divide that $100 million debt into smaller segments of, for example, $2,000. So, instead of 1–2 lenders lending the entire $100 million, 50,000 smaller lenders, such as other corporations or individuals, might each lend the corporation $2,000. Bonds allow many people to lend smaller portions to the corporation to help the corporation obtain the larger amount.

These smaller bond purchases occur as part of what is called a bond issuance. A corporation will announce a bond issuance to the public and invite interested parties to buy a bond, which is a sliver of the larger bond issuance. Think of bonds almost like crowdsourcing to obtain funding for a large loan. While not an exact comparison, it might help you visualize how bonds work. With crowdsourcing, an inventor has a large monetary need to create a prototype for an invention. Instead of finding a single person to provide that lump sum to the inventor, the inventor invites members of the public to contribute small amounts of money allowing the inventor to combine the smaller amounts of money to obtain the larger needed sum of money. The bond market is similar—a corporation seeking a large sum of money will invite members of the public to lend smaller amounts of money that in the aggregate provide the corporation the total amount needed.

It is sometimes difficult to understand the difference between a loan and a bond, so if you confuse them, rest assured you are in good company! Here are some quick references to help you distinguish.

- Loans and bonds are both debt instruments and have consistent terms: principal, issue date, maturity date, interest rate and other terms and conditions governing the debt.

- Loans for corporations are typically from banks and evidenced by a loan agreement.

- Loan agreements are contracts that can be assigned to another lender. Bonds are financial instruments that are highly negotiable and regularly traded on public markets.

- Bonds are issued by a corporation or government entity ("Issuer") and are purchased by individuals, other corporations or other government entities ("Bondholder"). Issuers sell bonds to bondholders for a fixed sum of money with a promise to repay the bondholder that fixed sum of money by a specified future date for a specified amount of interest.

- While a corporation might have a single bond issuance of millions of dollars, those purchasing the bonds are often required to purchase a minimum amount of bonds (maybe $1,000 or $2,000) and often in increments of $1,000. In other words, a bond issuer might issue $5 million of bonds, but require purchasers to purchase a minimum of $2,000 with any additional purchases required to be made in increments of $1,000.

- When bonds are publicly sold, the public is notified of the issuance and the specifics of the issuance using a prospectus. The prospectus might look something like this:

Sample Prospectus Supplement

<u>The Bond Offering</u>
The following is a brief summary of the terms and conditions of this Bond Offering. It does not contain all of the information needed to make an investment decision. To understand all of the terms and conditions of this debt offering, you should intentionally read this entire prospectus supplement as well as the accompanying prospectus and any other documents incorporated by reference in these documents.

Issuer	Widget Shoes, Inc.
Notes offered	$5,000,000,000 aggregate principal amount of Notes due in 2026 with an interest rate of 3%; $4,000,000,000 aggregate principal amount of Notes due in 2028 with an interest rate of 5%.
Original issue date	January 1, 2022
Maturity date	December 31, 2026 for the 3% Notes; December 31, 2028 for the 5% Notes;
Interest rate	3% per annum for the 2026 Notes; 5% per annum for the 2028 Notes;
Interest payment dates	Interest on all the Notes will be paid semi-annually on June 1 and December 31 of each calendar year, beginning on June 1, 2026, and on the applicable maturity date for each series of Notes.
Use of proceeds	The corporation intends to use the net proceeds from sales of the Notes, which is estimated to be approximately $9 billion, after deducting expenses from the bond issuance, for general corporate purposes, including repurchases of our common stock and payment of dividends under our program to return capital to shareholders, funding for working capital, capital expenditures, acquisitions and repayment of debt.
Denominations	The Notes will be issued only in minimum denominations of $2,000 and multiples of $1,000.
Governing law	Georgia

While this is an excerpt of what you would find in a prospectus, as you can see, the prospectus is designed to provide someone contemplating purchasing a bond with basic information on the principal being borrowed, the interest rates being paid, the maturity dates, how the bond proceeds will be used, and the minimum amount of bonds that must be purchased. In practice, a prospectus will be much longer with more detail about the bond issuance, the legal and market risks involved, and corporate information about the bond issuer. Remember that bonds are a form of debt sold to others in increment, allowing a corporation to obtain capital by borrowing smaller amounts of capital from a large number of individuals, corporations, and government entities.

Legal Highlights

Debt Analysis

When a lender issues a loan to a borrower, the lender makes the loan with the expectation that the lender will be repaid the principal and interest on the loan no later than the maturity date. To increase the likelihood of repayment, the lender will assess the riskiness of the loan.

To better understand this risk assessment, consider this from the perspective of the legal risks of the loan. As a future attorney, if you were drafting the loan agreement for your bank client who is making a loan to a corporation, what provisions would you insert into the loan agreement to help reduce your bank client's risk of not receiving repayment? What provisions would you include to protect against the corporation potentially suffering declining cash flow or increasing debt load? What about how to protect against the corporation taking on additional debt or becoming so insolvent that the corporation declares bankruptcy? What might you include in the loan agreement to address the risk of the corporation being sued and risking a sizable judgment claim against the corporation's assets?

Consider the following sample clauses:

Debt Service Coverage Ratio Clause. Clearly the bank will look at the corporation's primary source of repayment—the cash flow from the operating activities of the corporation. Thus, you might include a Debt Services Ratio clause requiring that the corporation's cash flow be a minimum amount every fiscal period or fiscal year. And, if the Debt Service Coverage Ratio falls below a level set forth in the loan agreement, you might include a provision allowing your bank client to demand that the loan be fully repaid immediately.

Liquidity Clause. To ensure that the corporation remains sufficiently liquid, you might include a clause requiring the corporation to maintain minimum working capital or a minimum Working Capital Ratio.

Encumbrance Clause. To ensure the corporation does not become laden with debt that could imperil the corporation's ability to repay your bank client, you might include a provision requiring the corporation to obtain your client's prior approval before taking on additional debt.

Bankruptcy Clause. To protect against the extensive authority of a bankruptcy court to unilaterally adjust your bank client's right to repayment of its loan, you might require the corporation to notify your bank client if the corporate borrower declares bankruptcy.

Major Litigation Clause. To protect against a judgment claim against the corporation's assets that might threaten the bank's repayment, you might include a provision that requires the corporation to notify the bank of any major litigation and include a provision allowing the bank to accelerate the loan and require immediate repayment in the event of major litigation.

To better understand how you might see these concepts in a loan agreement, consider the following sample provision from a sample loan agreement:

Subject to any notice requirement, grace period or right to cure that is specifically set forth in this Agreement, the occurrence of any one or more of the following events (each an "Event of Default") will constitute a default by the borrower, and the lender will be entitled to all rights and remedies available to it under the law and as set forth in this Agreement, including causing the outstanding balance of this Agreement to become immediately due and payable as of the date of the Event of Default.

(1) A breach, nonpayment, failure of performance or default by the borrower of any material covenant, term, condition, or provision of this Agreement, which is not cured within thirty (30) days notice from the lender.

(2) The sale, transfer, assignment, pledge or conveyance of the property or any portion thereof, without the prior written consent of the lender, which consent shall not be unreasonably withheld, conditioned or delayed.

(3) The insolvency or entry into bankruptcy of the borrower, or if there is commenced against the borrower any proceeding seeking the involuntary entry of the borrower into bankruptcy.

As you can see from the above example, as an attorney, you could draft a provision that makes the occurrence of certain events a breach of the loan agreement. Additionally, you could include certain remedies for such a breach, including acceleration of the loan agreement. In other words, you could accelerate the due date of the loan agreement requiring the borrower to repay the outstanding loan balance in full. This is an example of the role that attorneys play in helping clients protect themselves when seeking capital or lending capital.

C. Unsecured Debt and Secured Debt

Despite the protections listed above, the lender is likely still concerned about re-payment. If the lender is looking to the corporation's cash flow as the primary source of repayment, the lender is also likely looking to other secondary sources of repayment to minimize the riskiness of the debt. This is where the concept of unsecured debt and secured debt comes in.

1. Unsecured Debt

Unsecured debt occurs when a borrower does not pledge an asset as collateral to secure repayment of a debt. In other words, unsecured debt is when a corporate borrower has not pledged collateral for that debt. You are very familiar with unsecured debt. The easiest example is your credit card. As you undoubtedly know, credit cards allow you to make a charge on your credit card and repay that debt later. When you charge a purchase on your credit card, your credit card company pays the merchant from whom you made the purchase on your behalf and the credit card company then expects repayment from you by the "due date" on your credit card statement. Thus, the credit card company has extended debt to you, and with every credit card charge, you are increasing the debt you owe the credit card company. When you applied for the credit card, did you pledge an asset as collateral for the credit debt? No. Thus, credit cards are not just debt, they are unsecured debt. Similarly, think about your student loans—when you applied for those student loans, did you pledge collateral? No. Thus, your student loans are also unsecured debt.

2. Secured Debt

Secured debt means that the lender has taken a security interest in an asset as collateral for the debt. Put more simply, if the corporation does not repay the debt pursuant to the loan agreement, the lender has the right to liquidate the asset that the corporation has pledged to secure repayment of the debt and use those proceeds to repay the outstanding balance of the loan. For those of you who have bought a house or a car with a loan—did you have to pledge the house or the car as collateral for the debt? Yup. Thus, your mortgage loan and car loan are examples of secured debt.

Legal Highlights

Secured Debt

As an attorney, one of the ways we determine whether debt is secured or unsecured is to determine whether the borrower has signed a security agreement, or some similar document, pledging collateral for the loan. Additionally, we could also examine the loan agreement for any pledges of security.

Consider the following sample language from a sample loan agreement:

The Loan will be secured by a lien on the Real Property and any personalty and chattel on the Property. This Security Agreement executed by the parties shall serve as the security agreement required by the Uniform Commercial Code with respect to all furniture, fixtures, and equipment owned and to be acquired by borrower with respect to the Real Property as well as the Real Property as described in the attached Exhibit.

This language is a simplified example of the type of language that you will encounter for a secured loan. As you can see from the language, the loan is secured by the property as well as any personal property and chattel on the property. Thus, pursuant to the laws of foreclosure in the applicable jurisdiction, the lender has the right to enforce its lien against the real property to satisfy any unpaid balance due on the loan as well as use the laws of secured transactions to enforce its security interest in the personal property.

Collateral provides lenders with additional means of repayment should the borrower become unable or unwilling to repay the loan in accordance with the terms and conditions of the loan documents.

3. Lien Priority

Now that you have a better understanding of secured debt, think about what happens when there are multiple lenders with multiple loans all secured by the same property. Which lender gets the proceeds from the sale of the collateral and how much would each lender get? This question introduces you to the concept of lien priority. Let's do a thought exercise to understand the concept of lien priority:

Let's assume a corporation wants to purchase property. And, that property costs $200,000. The corporation tries to obtain a single $200,000 loan from a Bank to purchase the property, but no single lender is willing to provide a single $200,000 loan. However, the lenders are willing to offer smaller loans that the borrower can combine to purchase the $200,000 property. For example, the corporation obtains

- an $80,000 loan from Bank 1

- a $100,000 loan from Bank 2

- and a $20,000 loan from Bank 3

These three loans together total the $200,000 the corporation needs.

Graphically, it would look as follows:

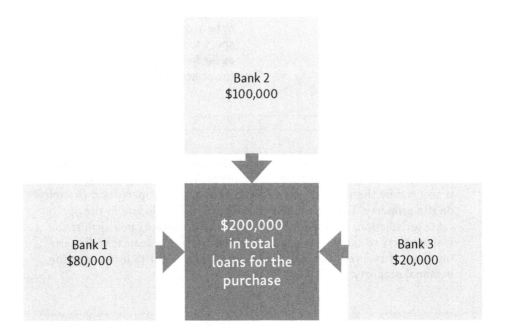

The borrower now has $200,000 in loans from three lenders to purchase the $200,000 property. All is well until the borrower defaults on the loan repayments. If the loans are secured, the lenders can go to court, foreclose on the property securing the loan, sell the property securing the loan, and use the proceeds from the sale to repay the outstanding loan balance. But, of the three lenders, which lender gets paid first? And, what happens if the total proceeds from the sale are less than the outstanding balance owed to the lenders—do all lenders receive the same amount of money or are lenders repaid in full in a certain order?

This is where the concept of priority comes in—priority determines which lender is repaid first, which lender is repaid second, which lender is repaid last, and which lender(s) might not be repaid at all. States have state-specific rules governing lien priority, and it is a subject that you can learn more about in Real Estate Transactions or Secured Transactions. While we will not cover this topic in further detail in this class, it is helpful to understand that collateral and lien priority are important factors in a lender's willingness to issue a loan and a bond purchaser's willingness to purchase a bond. Thus, from a business perspective, lien priority and a lender's ability to secure a higher lien priority are very important.

As transactional lawyers, it is important for us to understand these concepts as we draft the loan agreements and security agreements that will contain provisions setting forth how the rights and obligations of our lender or borrower clients are affected in the event of a default. As litigation lawyers, it is helpful for us to understand these concepts because we might be required to file suit, or defend against a suit, related to a defaulted loan.

D. Bond Redemption vs. Prepayment

As you know, loans and bonds are both required to be repaid no later than the maturity date set forth in the debt documents. However, it is not unusual for the borrower or bond issuer to seek to repay the debt prior to the maturity date. This introduces a couple of concepts: redemption and prepayment.

- Redemption occurs when a bond issuer (the borrower) repays a bond at or prior to its stated maturity date.

- Prepayment occurs when a borrower repays a loan prior to the maturity date stated in the loan agreement.

In either case, the documents for the bond issuance and the loan agreement will both state whether redemption or prepayment is permissible and whether such prepayment is subject to any early redemption or prepayment fees.

E. Chapter 8 Debt Analysis Exercises and Case Studies

Exercise 8.1—Widget Shoes Bond Prospectus

As you may recall from earlier in this chapter, when bonds are issued, they are typically issued with a prospectus. A prospectus is usually filed with the Securities and Exchange Commission and contains information about the bond issuance such as the corporation's plans for the proceeds from the offering, the corporation's financial condition and financial results, corporate history, corporate officers, and any other information that might be material to a potential bondholder. To familiarize yourself with these concepts, read through the following sample Prospectus Supplement and answer the questions that follow.

Widget Shoes Bond Prospectus Supplement

<u>The Bond Issuance</u>

The following is a brief summary of the terms and conditions of this Bond Issuance. It does not contain all of the information needed to make an investment decision. To understand all of the terms and conditions of this debt offering, you should intentionally read this entire prospectus supplement as well as the accompanying prospectus and any other documents incorporated by reference in these documents.

Issuer	Widget Shoes
Notes offered	$1,000,000,000 aggregate principal amount of 1.700% Notes due 2024;
	$1,200,000,000 aggregate principal amount of 1.800% Notes due 2025;
	$1,300,000,000 aggregate principal amount of 2.000% Notes due 2026;
	$1,400,000,000 aggregate principal amount of 2.200% Notes due 2027; and
	$1,500,000,000 aggregate principal amount of 2.300% Notes due 2028.
Original issue date	January 1, 2020
Maturity date	December 31, 2024 for the 1.700% Notes;
	December 31, 2025 for the 1.800% Notes;
	December 31, 2026 for the 2.00% Notes;
	December 31, 2027 for the 2.200% Notes; and
	December 31, 2028 for the 2.300% Notes.
Interest rate	1.700% per annum for the 2024 Notes;
	1.800% per annum for the 2025 Notes;
	2.000% per annum for the 2026 Notes;
	2.200% per annum for the 2027 Notes; and
	2.300% per annum for the 2028 Notes.
Interest payment dates	Interest on all the Notes will be paid semi-annually on June 1 and December 31 of each year, beginning on June 1, 2020, and on the applicable maturity date for each series of Notes.

Optional redemption	Prior to (i) with respect to the 2024 Notes, the maturity date of such Notes, (ii) with respect to the other Notes, one month prior to the maturity date of such Notes, such series of Notes may be redeemed at the issuer's option, at any time in whole or from time to time in part, at a redemption price as calculated by the issuer, equal to the greater of:
	100% of the principal amount of the notes being redeemed; or
	the sum of the present values of the remaining scheduled payments of principal and interest on the notes being redeemed at a rate equal to the sum of the applicable Treasury Rate plus 10 basis points.
Use of proceeds	We intend to use the net proceeds from sales of the Notes, which we estimate will be approximately $6 billion, after deducting underwriting discounts and our offering expenses, for general corporate purposes, including repurchases of our common stock and payment of dividends under our program to return capital to shareholders, funding for working capital, capital expenditures, acquisitions and repayment of debt.
Denominations	The Notes will be issued only in minimum denominations of $2,000 and integral multiples of $1,000 in excess thereof.
Governing law	Illinois

Questions for Exercise 8.1—Widget Shoes Bond Prospectus

1. Do you notice a correlation between the interest rate of the debt and the maturity date of the debt? If so, why do you think that is?

2. Your client asks you to review the Widget Shoes prospectus and draft a letter to his investment advisor about purchasing Widget Shoes bonds maturing in 2026. She wants you to reference the interest rate on that debt. What is the applicable interest rate?

3. How much capital does Widget Shoes project it will generate from this bond issuance?

4. Are the Widget Shoes bonds redeemable?

Chapter 8 Highlights

- Debt is a legally binding contract that is subject to contract law analysis and, potentially, securities law.
- Debt is generally comprised of loans and bonds.
- Debt will be either unsecured (no collateral) or secured debt. Secured debt with multiple lenders will generally require a determination of lien priority.
- The loan agreement will have many contractual provisions designed to protect against risk to the lender.
- The lender will assess an interest charge to the borrower as the cost of utilizing the lender's funds.

Nine

Equity Analysis

- This is a companion chapter to Chapter 8.
- This chapter provides an overview of equity. It explains the definition of equity—common stock and preferred stock—and the legal differences between them.
- This chapter also includes a business analysis of equity and the business difference between equity and debt.
- In this chapter you will also find a case study of an interview with an attorney working as in-house counsel for a venture capital firm to enable you to hear perspectives from a practicing business attorney.

A. What Is Equity?

As we have discussed, there are two major sources of capital—debt and equity. When individual or corporate investors purchase shares in a corporation, those investors are providing the corporation "equity." Equity broadly refers to the ownership interest investors receive in exchange for purchasing shares in a corporation.

As you have discovered by now, terminology in finance does not have the same exact precision as it does in law. When someone says to you "negligence," you immediately think of the primary four elements of negligence—duty, breach, causation and damages. However, finance terminology often does not have that same specificity. In finance, when someone says "equity," it could mean:

- Home Equity. The equity that someone has in their home (the difference between the value of the home and the amount of money the owner owes on the home).

- Owner's Equity on the Balance Sheet. It could also mean the owner's equity section of the Balance Sheet showing the amount of funds contributed by the corporation's owners plus the amount of net profit retained in the corporation in retained earnings (remember that one from Chapter 2?).

- A Form of Capital. Equity could also mean selling an ownership stake in the corporation to an investor in exchange for cash. In an oversimplified transaction, this would be reflected on the Balance Sheet by an increase in the balance in the cash account and an increase in the balance in the owner's equity section of the Balance Sheet. In the owner's equity section of the Balance Sheet, you would see the "common stock" and "additional paid-in-capital" accounts reflect the amount the corporation received from the sale of common shares—also called equity—to investors. Once those investors purchase the shares, the investors also become co-owners in the corporation.

In finance parlance, (i) the investors are receiving "equity" in the corporation, or in alternative parlance, (ii) the investors now "have an equity stake," or (iii) are "taking an equity position" in the corporation. These investors are purchasing shares in the corporation at an agreed upon purchase price with the hope that the investment will be able to generate a profit.

Since finance terminology does not have the same precision as legal terminology, you have to look at context to know and understand which definition of equity is intended. Yes, that will likely be frustrating to those of you who like the certainty of legal meaning, but with more exposure to finance concepts and terminology, you will be able to discuss business issues with your clients and colleagues and feel like the insider you will become!

Alright, let's get into it. You should recall that debt is a legally binding contract providing legal rights to repayment, whereas equity generally does not have those types of legal protections, which makes repayment of equity a riskier proposition.

For-profit businesses generally operate on a basic principle of risk vs. return—the higher the risk, the higher the return. Thus, if equity is a riskier investment because it does not have a legally binding obligation of repayment of the investment, equity investors will demand a higher return from that investment to compensate the investor for that risk.

Let's do a thought exercise together to think through these concepts:

Imagine, if you will, your friend who started Widget Shoes asking you to invest your hard-earned money from your first legal job in your friend's new venture. Your first thought will be of how long you waited to finally have money in your bank account, so you'll be hard pressed to relinquish those precious dollars. But your friend explains to you that he's just sure that the corporation will be successful if just given the opportunity to thrive. So, you agree to listen...skeptically. What are some of the questions you might have about the investment and the ability to get your very precious money repaid to you? You might ask and he might answer....

- How much money do you need?

  - Oh, about $5,000.

- Ok, well when will I get my money returned?

  - We will repay you when the business makes enough profit to have some extra cash.

- Uhmm, "extra cash"?!? How does one have extra cash? Isn't all cash important?!?

  - Well, yeah, of course. But the business will need to have sufficient cash to pay its bills and operate, so we are thinking that if we have cash left over after the business pays its bills and keeps enough cash to operate, then we will have that "extra cash" to return money to our investors.

- Investors—plural? There are others? Well, which of us gets our money back first?

  - Good question. I'm thinking whoever provides us the largest amount. But I can see your concern....

- Let's put a pin in that for a sec. How can I be sure my money will be used for the business?

  - C'mon, we've been friends for a long time. I wouldn't do that to you.

- Yah-hunh. How can I be sure my money will be used for the business!?

  - Ok, fiiiiine. As a condition of your investment, we will agree that you will receive a copy of our quarterly financial statements and we will include you in discussions of major decisions.

- That sounds better, but that sounds like you're going to decide what to tell me as opposed to me deciding what I need to hear. Tell ya' what—I think I want to be involved on the front end of decisions and have a voice in those decisions. I think a seat on the Board of Directors will enable me to do that.

  - Wow, no trust here, hunh?

- To use the old phrase—trust but verify. You're not asking for a friendly loan but instead an investment in a business, so I need to make sure my investment is protected.

  - I guess I can see that. What else do you want to know?

- Glad you asked! I have a few more questions! (i) How has the corporation performed so far? (ii) Does the company have many competitors which might impede sales? (iii) Tell me about your customer list and marketing plans. (iv) When will the company do that thing I hear about on the news for newer companies. I think it's called an IPO? ...

Legal Highlights

Equity Analysis

As the attorney, it will be your responsibility to be familiar with many of these concepts, as you will be required to draft the Investor Agreement from the terms set forth in the Term Sheet.

These are all very reasonable questions and are similar to the types of questions that an investor will ask a company prior to investing. Thus, it is not unusual for an investor to demand and/or negotiate many of the following terms of an equity investment. These terms of a proposed transaction are often presented in what is called a Term Sheet. Some of these terms include:[1]

- Board of Directors seat
- Dividends (cumulative or non-cumulative)
- Employee Stock Options

  - A provision requiring any employees who have a right to purchase the company's shares to do so only after the employee has worked with the company for a specified period of time.

---

1. Some terms are from the National Venture Capitalist Association Model Legal Documents.

- Lock-Up Agreements

  - Agreement whereby new investors agree to refrain from selling their shares for an agreed-upon period of time after the company's initial public offering of shares.

- Management and Information Rights

  - Agreement whereby the company will provide investors periodic financial statements (fiscal month, quarter or annual), information about the company's financial projections, and regular information about new debt or equity investments.

- Matters Requiring Investor Approval

  - An agreement prohibiting the company from engaging in specified activities without the prior approval of the investor.

- Non-Compete Agreements

  - A provision requiring the company to obtain non-compete agreements from some of the company's founders or high-ranking executives, in jurisdictions where it's permissible.

- Non-Disclosure Agreements

  - An agreement that the company will require specified employees to enter into an agreement prohibiting that employee from disclosing certain proprietary information to others.

- Priority upon Liquidation of the Company

  - An agreement that specified persons will be repaid their investment ahead of other shareholders, as permitted by state law.

- Reimbursement of Investor's Investment Expenses

  - An agreement that the company will reimburse the investor for expenses incurred by the investor to make the equity investment. Such expenses could include legal fees, filing fees or advisor financial fees.

- Right to Participate in Future Equity Investments

  - An agreement giving investors the right to purchase additional shares from the company.

- Vesting Requirements

  - A provision requiring the company's founders to meet specified metrics or tenure with the company before the founders are permitted to sell their shares in the company.

B. Preferred Stock and Common Stock

There are two types of shares of equity—preferred stock (also called preferred shares) and common stock (also called common shares). Both types of shares provide the investor with an equity ownership in the corporation, however, each state's corporations statute provides owners of preferred and common stock (preferred shareholders or common shareholders) with different rights. Thus, while you will learn some general differences here, it is important to note that these differences are not universal across states, so be sure to carefully review the applicable state's corporations statute to determine the rights and obligations of preferred and common stockholders.

Generally, preferred stock provides preferred shareholders with preferences in these areas:

1. Dividends
2. Liquidation
3. Voting
   - Common shareholders have the statutory right to vote for the Board of Directors

Now, what does all this mean? Let's start with dividends.

1. Dividends

You might recall from our discussion on Income Statements that dividends are a corporation's way of returning corporate profit back to shareholders. At the end of a fiscal period, a corporation's Board of Directors might "declare a dividend." For example, on April 28, 2021, Apple declared a dividend of $0.22 per share for its shareholders.[2] This means that the affected shareholders received a cash payment of $0.22 for each share they own. Granted, that doesn't sound like a lot of money, but remember a couple of items—(i) Apple declares multiple dividends per year, and (ii) Apple has approximately 17 billion outstanding shares. For context, in fiscal year-end 2020, Apple declared over $14 billion in dividends. So, as you can see, while the per share dividend may not seem very much for a single dividend payment, in totality, it is actually a fairly healthy sum.

If a corporation declares a dividend and has preferred and common shareholders, the question then becomes—who gets paid their dividends first? This is where the difference in the two classes of stock becomes relevant. Corporations statutes might say that preferred shareholders will have statutory preference in the payment of dividends. In other words, if the corporation does declare a dividend, preferred shareholders, if there are any, must be paid first. After preferred shareholders are paid their dividends, common shareholders can be paid a dividend. In this regard, you can see a clear preference for owning preferred stock. Let's look at the other differences and see if this preference withstands further examination.

---

2. *Dividend History*, APPLE, https://investor.apple.com/dividend-history/default.aspx (last visited Aug. 1, 2021).

2. Liquidation

While most corporations begin operations with the idea that the corporation will be around for decades, there are many corporations that voluntarily or involuntarily cease operations. When that happens, the corporation's bills must be paid with whatever assets the corporation has. If there is money remaining after paying all of the corporation's liabilities and if there are preferred and common shareholders, there must be guidance as to who is paid first. Corporations statutes will provide this guidance. Often times, preferred shareholders will be repaid their investment and then, if money remains, the entirety of the remainder goes to the common shareholders. Think about that—preferred shareholders receive what they are owed, but common shareholders receive all that is left after that. So, if there is little money remaining after liquidation, common shareholders will receive very little, if anything, so preferred shareholders would have the advantage. However, if there is a lot remaining after liquidation, common shareholders may have the advantage.

3. Voting

Voting rights is an issue that is often persuasive to investors determining whether to purchase preferred or common stock. Generally, common shareholders have the right to elect the Board of Directors. Why would one care, you might ask? Since the Board of Directors is elected by shareholders, the Board of Directors is thus directly answerable to shareholders. That is a powerful tool for an investor to have to protect their investment.

C. Chapter 9 Equity Analysis Exercises and Case Studies

Exercise 9.1—Preferred Stock vs. Common Stock

This exercise is a legal exercise. This is to allow you to read statutory excerpts so you can directly experience how equity ownership is written in law.

Read the following excerpts from two corporate statutes to see the law behind the differences between preferred stock and common stock:

Preferred stock's ability to have preference in dividends (Delaware corporate statute—emphasis added)[3]

(c) <u>The holders of preferred</u> or special <u>stock</u> of any class or of any series thereof <u>shall be entitled to receive dividends</u> at such rates, on such condi-

---

3. Many corporations are incorporated in Delaware, so many corporations must adhere to Delaware law. Thus, Delaware law is included as a reference.

tions and at such times <u>as shall be stated in the certificate of incorporation</u> or in the resolution or resolutions providing for the issue of such stock adopted by the board of directors as hereinabove provided, <u>payable in preference to,</u> or in such relation to, <u>the dividends payable on any other class</u> or classes or of any other series <u>of stock,</u> and <u>cumulative or noncumulative as shall be so stated</u> and expressed. <u>When dividends upon the preferred</u> and special <u>stocks,</u> if any, to the extent of the preference to which such stocks are entitled, <u>shall have been paid</u> or declared and set apart for payment, <u>a dividend on the remaining class</u> or classes or series <u>of stock may then be paid out of the remaining assets of the corporation available for dividends</u> as elsewhere in this chapter provided.[4]

Preferred stock's ability to have preference in liquidation (Delaware statute—emphasis added)

(d) <u>The holders of the preferred</u> or special <u>stock</u> of any class or of any series thereof <u>shall be entitled to such rights upon the dissolution of,</u> or upon any distribution of <u>the assets of, the corporation as shall be stated in the certificate of incorporation</u> or in the resolution or resolutions providing for the issue of such stock adopted by the board of directors as hereinabove provided.[5]

Common stock prohibited from having preference in dividends or in liquidation (Illinois corporate statute—emphasis added)

Sec. 6.05. Authorized shares. <u>Each corporation shall have power to create and issue the number of shares stated in its articles of incorporation. Such shares may be divided into one or more classes, including classes of common shares, any or all of which classes may consist of shares with such</u> designations, <u>preferences,</u> qualifications, limitations, restrictions, and such special or relative rights <u>as shall be stated in the articles of incorporation; provided, however, that common shares may have no preference over any other shares with respect to distribution of assets upon liquidation or with respect to payment of dividends.</u>[6]

As you can see, by statute, Illinois prohibits corporations from providing common shareholders priority over other shares in the distribution of assets upon liquidation of the corporation or in the payment of dividends. It is important for you as an attorney to review the applicable state statute to properly advise your client about the rights and preferences of preferred and common shareholders.

---

4. Del. Code Ann. tit. 8, § 151(c) (2021).
5. Del. Code Ann. tit. 8, § 151(d) (2021).
6. 805 Ill. Comp. Stat. 5/6.05 (2021).

Case Study 9.2—Lawyer's Role in Equity Transactions

To help you have a better understanding of the analysis involved in determining whether a corporation solicits equity for capital, and the attorney's role, please read the interview below with Nicole Simmons, General Counsel of Peregrade Ventures.

1. Describe your business and your role:

   I am the General Counsel at a Single Family Office. Our organization functions much like a Private Equity and Venture Capital firm (PEVC) (i.e., we source, do due diligence, and make investments of capital), but we also operate an entrepreneurial segment we refer to as "New Business Creation" (NBC), which functions much like a startup incubator program. In my role, I develop and support the legal strategy and transactions for all of our business segments, including the PEVC group and NBC group, with a focus on aligning with our organization's Investment Policy Statement (IPS). I also serve as one of 3 members of the firm's Investment Committee, on which I have the opportunity to fully analyze the due diligence our team has conducted and cast a vote whether we should deploy capital.

2. For those law students new to business, explain why a company might opt for equity financing instead of debt financing.

   The decision to fundraise through equity or debt financing typically arises fairly early in a startup's lifecycle, within the first 1–3 years. Although every startup is unique in its own way, in my experience, generally founders will prefer to seek to raise funds through an equity round for 2 primary reasons:

   1. *The prospective investor has subject matter and business expertise specific or complementary to the startup's core business (e.g., the startup is a consumer-packaged-goods company that brings on investors with supply chain expertise). When a founder exchanges some equity (and by extension, control) of the business for funds, it can often be based on the need for business synergies, partnership, and advisory input from the prospective investor, who may be uniquely positioned to help the startup scale. This type of engagement often balances in favor of the startup granting a share of the ownership to the prospective investor; and/or*

Definition

Founders

Founders usually refer to the individual founders of a start-up company.

2. *The startup's risk profile may be such that the founder or management team do not want to take on risk of repaying a debt—when a startup fundraises through an equity financing, a share of the ownership is absorbed by the investor, and while there may be some preferred return of capital in the equity financing, typically the startup does not have a legal obligation to pay back the investor at a specified time or maturity date, as is usually the case in a debt financing. Additionally, oftentimes in debt financing, the investor will require security for the debt, such as the founder's personal assets.*

3. What are some of the major legal challenges new companies face in obtaining capital?

   From the startup perspective, one of the biggest challenges I have observed in early-stage companies is meeting the contingencies of investors before funding occurs. With early stage, unproven businesses, many times investors will have fairly robust metrics and milestones (or Key Performance Indicators) the startup must meet or achieve before the investor funds part or all of the investment (e.g., in a tech startup, an investor will only fund in tranches and each tranche of funding is dependent upon acquiring a certain number of new customers or users). This "installment" type of approach can make it very unpredictable for startups to forecast budget, cash flow, etc. where the metrics must be met before investors agree to provide funds. This comes up with both equity and debt financings.

> **Definition**
>
> *Subscription Agreement*
>
> Subscription Agreements are purchase agreements between a corporation and initial investors to sell shares.

4. What are the legal drawbacks, if any, for using equity?

   From the startup perspective, giving up a portion of the ownership and control of the company can be a material drawback in and of itself. In my experience, this can be particularly troublesome for startups where the investor is active and wants to get engaged in the day-to-day operation of the business.

5. What is the attorney's role in closing a deal for equity financing?

   While it varies greatly depending on the relative bargaining power of the investor and the startup (e.g., how many other investors are competing to invest in the startup?), where the investor takes a leading position in the fundraising round, investor counsel's role typically includes: (a) due diligence of the legal state of the startup (reviewing the company's organizational documents, contracts, liabilities, etc.), (b) alignment and sometimes drafting legal opinions regarding alignment with investment thesis or policy, (c) preparation of a term sheet outlining the terms upon which the investor will provide funds, (d) negotiation of terms favorable to the investor, and (e) drafting of definitive subscription agreements or side letters applicable to the investment.

6. Any words of wisdom for young lawyers working with corporate clients?

Understand your client's business. Spending time getting to know the practical and operational components of your client's business is so valuable and informative to your ability to represent and truly create differentiated value for your client and will empower you to do your best, most effective legal work.

Legal Highlights

Equity Analysis

Note that both Nicole Simmons, here, and Dennis Beresford from the Worldcom case study, both emphasize the importance of an attorney learning their client's business.

As an attorney, we add value when we can translate our client's business needs and concerns to legal issue spotting. We can only do that by taking the time to learn about our client's business concerns, their business operations, and their financial goals. Being an attorney is not just about knowing the law but knowing how to apply the law to client needs.

D. Equity Investment Payoff

Broadly speaking, investors in a corporation earn money from an equity investment in one of three ways: (i) dividends, (ii), equity appreciation, and (iii) liquidation.

1. Dividends

The investors can earn money if, during the time the investors own the shares, the corporation generates enough net profit to return some of that net profit to the shareholders (the investors) as dividends.

For example:

Cash Outflow

Jan 1, 2020 share purchase price (cash outflow):	$50 per share

Cash Inflow

Jul 1, 2020 dividend payment:	$2 per share
Dec 31, 2020 dividend payment:	$2 per share
Jul 2, 2021 dividend payment:	$1 per share
Dec 31, 2021 dividend payment:	$1 per share
Jul 2, 2022 dividend payment:	$1 per share
Dec 31, 2022 dividend payment:	<u>$1 per share</u>
Total Cash Inflow	$8 per share
Net Cash Flow	−$42 per share

2. Equity Appreciation

In this scenario, investors purchase shares at an agreed upon price. With that purchase, equity investors are projecting that at some point in the future, the investors will be able to sell those shares at a price higher than what the investors paid for those shares.

For example:

Cash Outflow

Jan 1, 2020 share *purchase* price:	$50 per share

Cash Inflow

Jul 1, 2020 dividend payment:	$2 per share
Dec 31, 2020 dividend payment:	$2 per share
Jul 2, 2021 dividend payment:	$1 per share
Dec 31, 2021 dividend payment:	$1 per share
Jul 2, 2022 dividend payment:	$1 per share
Dec 31, 2022 dividend payment:	$1 per share
Jun 30, 2023 share *sale* price:	<u>$62 per share</u>
Total Cash Inflow	$70 per share
Net Cash Flow	$20 per share

3. Liquidation of Company

The investors can also earn money if, during the time the investors own the shares, the corporation ceases operations and liquidates all of the corporation's assets. Let's think about this for a bit. As discussed earlier, if a corporation closes down, can it just close down and the owners take all the cash from the corporation's bank account and move to Aruba? Of course not. The corporation must pay off all of its creditors first, and then, any assets that remain can be distributed to the owners (shareholders).

Think about the Balance Sheet—the left side has assets and the right side has liabilities. An easy way to view the Balance Sheet is to remember that the right side of the Balance Sheet has a claim on the left side of the Balance Sheet. So, a simplified way of thinking about a corporate liquidation is that the corporation must liquidate the assets on the left side of the Balance Sheet to repay the creditors shown on the right side of the Balance Sheet, and then the corporation can distribute the remainder to the shareholders—preferred shareholders first, if any, and then common shareholders, subject to state statutory or judicial requirements.

E. Chapter 9 Equity Analysis Exercises and Case Studies cont'd

Exercise 9.3—Equity Analysis

1. What are major legal differences between debt and equity?

2. Why would a corporate borrower choose debt as a source of capital instead of equity? Conversely, why would a corporate borrower choose equity as a source of capital instead of debt?

3. In the event of a corporate liquidation, if a corporation has creditors and common and preferred shareholders, generally in what order will each group receive a distribution of liquidated assets?

Exercise 9.4—Widget Shoes Equity Prospectus

Although the business team will analyze the financial aspects of a public offering of shares, attorneys are very involved in the preparation of the prospectus in advance of a public offering of shares. Thus, it is important that attorneys learn the business concepts so that you can prepare a prospectus if you are a securities lawyer. For those of you thinking that this might not be relevant because you want to be a litigator, consider this—what happens if your senior partner asks you to help prepare a brief in response to a shareholder's lawsuit against one of your corporate clients? For those of you who want to do estate planning, envision a client asking you to review a prospectus of a corporation whose stock your client is contemplating including in the client's estate plan. Whichever type of law you practice, it is important to have some familiarity with equity investments in corporations.

To help get you comfortable with these concepts, review the excerpt of a sample equity offering and answer the questions that follow.

Widget Shoes Equity Offering Prospectus

The following is a description of our capital stock from our Articles of Incorporation and Bylaws that will be in effect on the closing date of this offering. The descriptions of the common stock and preferred stock reflect our capital structure that will be in effect on the closing of this offering.

On the closing of this offering, our Articles of Incorporation will provide for one class of common stock. In addition, our Articles of Incorporation will authorize shares of preferred stock, the rights, preferences, and privileges of which may be designated from time to time by our board of directors.

On the closing of this offering, our capital stock will consist of 5,000,000,000 authorized shares, all with a par value of $0.00001 per share, of which: 4 billion shares are designated common stock; and 1 billion shares are designated preferred stock.

As of December 31, 2020, there were 1 billion shares of our common stock and 500 million shares of redeemable convertible preferred stock outstanding.

Our outstanding capital stock was held by approximately 2,000 stockholders of record as of December 31, 2020.

Common Stock

Voting Rights

Holders of our common stock are entitled to one vote per share on any matter submitted to our stockholders. Our Articles of Incorporation will not provide for cumulative voting for the election of directors.

Economic Rights

Dividends and Distributions. Subject to preferences that may apply to any shares of the outstanding redeemable convertible preferred stock, the holders of common stock will be entitled to share equally, identically and ratably, on a per share basis, with respect to any dividend or distribution of cash or property paid or distributed by the corporation.

Liquidation Rights. Upon the corporation's liquidation, dissolution or winding-up, the holders of common stock will be entitled to share equally, identically and ratably in all assets remaining after the payment of any liabilities, liquidation preferences and accrued or declared but unpaid dividends, if any, with respect to any outstanding redeemable convertible preferred stock.

Questions for Exercise 9.4—Widget Shoes Equity Prospectus

1. According to the offering prospectus, how many outstanding shares did the corporation have as of December 31, 2020?

2. Your client is thinking of purchasing 1,000 shares of common stock from this offering. If your client completes this purchase, how many votes would your client have?

3. If your client purchased 1,000 shares of common stock from this offering and if afterwards, the corporation paid $2 per share in a dividend, based just on the information in the excerpt above, how much would your client receive in dividends?

Chapter 9 Highlights

- An equity investment is an investor purchasing shares in a corporation with the overarching goal of making a profit on this purchase.

- There are two major types of equity with characteristics determined by state statute.
  - Preferred Stock
    - Usually has preference in liquidation and dividends
    - Usually, no statutory right to vote for Board of Directors
  - Common Stock
    - Statutory right to vote for Board of Directors
    - Residual claim on assets

- Equity investors make money from their equity investment in a corporation primarily by equity appreciation, receipt of dividends, and upon the corporation's liquidation.

Ten

Capital Markets and Valuation

- Now that you have a basic understanding of financial statements, time value of money and capital, this chapter will help you understand the basics of the capital markets.
- This chapter will begin with a review of the principle of time value of money and use that to help you understand a major component of valuation.
- The chapter will then explain valuation principles for equity (stocks) and debt (bonds).

Imagine Widget Shoes has performed well. Its revenue has exceeded its financial projections, its gross profit margin has remained above 80% for the past three fiscal quarters, its operating expenses have remained less than 30% of gross profit, its revenue has grown a steady 3% for the past three fiscal years, and its net profit has been high enough to allow the corporation to declare a $1 cash dividend per share for the past two years (aren't you excited that you were able to—at least mostly—follow this sentence! Congrats on that!).

Given the corporation's financial performance, the corporation now wants to expand and open two more manufacturing facilities. But that will take a lot of money. Widget Shoes is performing well, but not well enough to have sufficient cash for the expansion. Without the cash, the corporation cannot expand. From where should Widget Shoes obtain the needed cash?[1]

In circumstances such as these, companies such as Widget Shoes will seek capital from the capital markets. Now, when I discuss "capital markets," no I don't mean like an open-air flea market or even a single building. Capital markets is a term that refers to a process rather than a place. Capital markets refers to the process a corporation goes through to find, get reviewed and approved for, and receive, capital. It refers to the process of obtaining equity investments from investors as well as the process of obtaining debt from private lenders by obtaining a loan or by issuing bonds.

Graphically, you can think of obtaining capital from the capital markets as follows:

---

1. When asking about obtaining cash for operations, you will frequently hear this referred to as "capital." So, when you hear the term capital in business (note it is spelled with an "a" not an "o"), know that the speaker is generally referring to obtaining cash either from debt or equity which we discussed in a previous chapter.

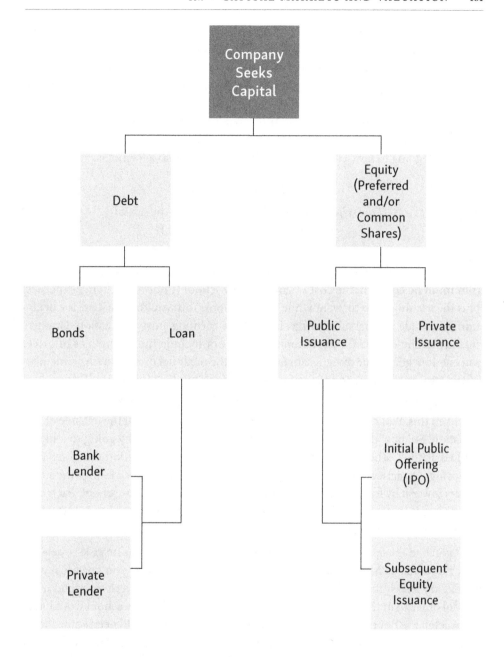

A. Risk vs. Return

Let us consider this concept of risk for a moment. Risk is quantifiable, and many people spend many years contemplating the concept and cost of risk. You intuitively know it as well. Think about your decision to go to law school. Since law school is not free, you decided to invest in law school and assume the riskiness of that investment. You (hopefully) contemplated—though not likely quantified—how much law school

would cost to attend and how much you needed to generate in income upon graduation to make law school worth the investment. You likely recognized that there is
some risk to that decision—what if you don't get the salary you need; what if you are
unable to work in your preferred practice area; what if you are not able to live in your
preferred location? That is an analysis of risk. The last two are more intangible risks.
The first one is the only one of these three that is a financial risk—the riskiness that
your salary post-graduation is less than the salary you could have generated without
the cost of going to law school. So, let us try to put this into a formula:

Earnings post-graduation ≥
(Law school tuition + living expenses in law school
+ loss of income during law school)

In other words, your earnings post-graduation would need to exceed, or at a
minimum be equal to, the cost of going to law school (tuition and living expenses)
plus the earnings you forwent while in law school. You would evaluate this calculation to include the riskiness of receiving those earnings post-graduation. Granted,
this is just the financial calculation and does not include the intangibles of career
satisfaction, goal achievement satisfaction, or the personal pride of being a member
of the legal profession, and those factors are much harder to quantify. This analysis
is simply about the financial impact and riskiness of this decision.

Given this, you clearly would want to decrease the riskiness of the left side of that
equation. So, how do you lower that risk? Some lower the risk by going to a higher
ranked school, others lower it by going to a lower cost school, others lower it by
choosing a practice area where they have a higher likelihood of being hired, and
others lower it by focusing on obtaining a higher GPA rank in law school. Each of us
has different levers we can press to lower the riskiness of our decision to attend law
school, but that risk exists for all of us.

If you had the opportunity to go to law school where there was no risk—meaning
that there was a risk-free law school you could attend—would you go? Most of us
would say yes, of course! I mean, why not, right? So, if you were to attend a law
school other than that risk-free law school, the non-risk-free law school would need
to sweeten the pot to get you to attend. In other words, you would need some incentive to attend a law school other than the risk-free law school; you would need some
incentive to persuade you to take on that additional risk. Well, investors think similarly—investors require some additional incentive or premium to invest in an investment that is not a risk-free investment. And that incentive is part of the cost of
equity for the investor; the investor is going to require some incentive—in the world
of finance that would be a higher return—to invest in an investment other than a
risk-free investment.

1. Risk-Free Investments in American Finance

In American finance, there is only one investment that is considered a risk-free investment and that is the bonds issued by the US government. These are known as US Treasuries. You may have heard them referred to as T-Bills, T-Notes, and T-Bonds, but these are bonds issued and backed by the full faith and credit of the US government. The US government has not defaulted on its debt, so US Treasuries are considered, in American finance, a risk-free investment. So, the return on US Treasuries is considered the "risk-free rate." Thus, any investment other than US Treasuries is inherently a riskier investment, and thus, an investor would require a return higher than the then current market rate of return on a US Treasury.

B. Cost of Capital

When a corporation seeks capital, that corporation must find a capital provider to provide that capital. That capital provider is not likely to provide that capital for free, so the corporation must pay a charge for that capital. As discussed in Chapter 8, the cost of debt is the interest charged by the lender as determined by the lender's interest rate. Let's dig a little deeper into a corporation's cost of debt. We will discuss the cost of equity a little later in this chapter.

1. Cost of Debt

If a corporation wants to use debt to raise capital, the corporation must determine what return the corporation must offer to attract lenders willing to lend capital. This section will review the cost a corporation must incur to obtain debt. In other words, what is a corporation's cost of debt? You know that interest is the charge that a borrower must pay to compensate the lender for lending capital to the corporation. This section will discuss whether the interest charged on a corporation's debt is truly the corporation's cost of debt. Are there other factors that would impact how to calculate the cost of debt to the corporation? You know us professors rarely ask purely rhetorical questions, so since I'm asking these questions, clearly there is another factor to consider. So, here goes—

The federal government, for various policy reasons, allows a corporation to deduct its interest costs from that corporation's taxable income. Thus, a corporation's taxable income is reduced by the amount of a corporation's interest costs. This means that when a corporation pays interest that is then deducted from that corporation's taxable income, that corporation saves money in taxes. Review the chart below to see the financial benefit of deducting interest:

Financial benefit of interest deduction (assuming a 20% corporate tax rate):

Without Interest Expense		With Interest Expense	
Operating Income	$100,000	Operating Income	$100,000
Less: Interest Expense	$0	*Less: Interest Expense*	$10,000
Taxable Income =	$100,000	Taxable Income =	$90,000
Tax Rate	20%	Tax Rate	20%
Tax to be paid =	$20,000	Tax to be paid =	$18,000

Difference in tax to be paid = $2,000

As you can see, the interest deduction reduces the corporation's tax liability by $2,000 ($20,000 less $18,000). Thus, the interest paid is not the corporation's actual cost of debt. The corporation's true cost of debt is $8,000 calculated as follows: the corporation's interest costs (here, $10,000) less the financial benefit of deducting the corporation's interest expense from the corporation's taxable income (here $2,000).

> **Legal Highlights**
>
> *Capital Markets*
>
> As an attorney, understanding this concept will provide you with a better understanding of your clients' Income Statements and help you better understand why debt might be an attractive means of raising capital compared to equity.

2. Debt Valuation

Now that you have a basic understanding of the business and legal aspect of debt, let us think about how to value that debt. Debt, as you may know, has cash value. Let's think about what that means. How does a lender receive cash for debt that is owed to the lender?

- One obvious option is that the borrower can simply repay the debt to the lender. That means that the borrower pays cash to the lender to repay the debt that the borrower owes to the lender. In that instance, the borrower transfers cash to the lender and the amount of the borrower's debt balance thus decreases.

- A less obvious option for the lender receiving cash for the debt occurs when the lender sells the lender's right to repayment of the debt to another lender. You might have heard this in finance circles referred to as the lender "selling the debt". Think back to your contracts class: when one party to a contract wants to transfer its rights in a contract, that party can assign the contract to a third party. That same option exists with debt, because as you may recall, debt is a contract. The lender assigns the right to receive payment for the debt contract to a third party in exchange for a cash payment. Consider the following example: have you ever wondered why the debt you owed to the doctor's office for a doctor's visit from college that you've *really* been meaning to repay is now being collected by some annoying company that keeps calling you and leaving less than pleasant messages on your voice mail? That is because the doctor's office, after being unable to collect the debt from you, sold that debt to a third party who now has the legal right to collect that debt from you directly. After the doctor's office sells that debt to the new company, when you finally repay that debt, you will not pay it to the doctor's office. Instead, you would pay it to the new company because the new company now would be the entity with the legal right to repayment.

So, if a lender is selling its debt, the investor who is purchasing the debt must determine how much to pay for that debt. Thus, the investor will need to determine the cash value of that debt. There are several factors to consider such as:

- Return on Investment
  - How much cash does the investor expect to receive for that debt?
- Risk
  - What is the borrower's likelihood of repayment?
- Term
  - How long will the investor hold onto the debt? Will the investor hold onto the debt until the maturity date of the debt, or will the investor sell that debt before the maturity date?

All these factors will impact the cash value of the debt and thus determine how much an investor will be willing to pay to buy debt from a lender.

Now, let's go through an example of how to value debt by...bear with me now...calculating the present value of a bond's future stream of cash flows. Envision the following—you are a trusts and estates lawyer working with a client who wants a relatively safe investment for their retirement portfolio. Your client tells you that the client's financial advisor has recommended bonds. Your client provides you the information about the bonds so that you can draft information about beneficiaries for the client's estate documents. If you were to ask your client how much the client will pay for the bonds, the client might offer the following explanation of their process for determining a purchase price—"In essence, I figure out the total amount of cash I will receive from the bonds and then calculate how much that future stream of cash flows is worth in today's dollars. In other words, I determine how much the bond will pay me over the length of time I own the bonds and then use a discount rate to determine the present value of that future stream of cash flows." He sees you looking confused (maybe the same look you are virtually giving me now) and provides the following example—"Assume you are purchasing a bond that has the following:

> **Definition**
>
> *Coupon Rate*
>
> Coupon rate is the interest rate paid by the bond issuer to the bondholder. It is a bit of a dated term as it refers to a paper, detachable 'coupon' that the bondholder used to use to obtain interest payments. While paper delivery of bonds have been replaced with electronic delivery, the term 'coupon rate' is still often used to refer to the interest rate of a bond.

- Face Value (principal amount) = $1,000
- Coupon Rate (assume annual dividend payments) = 10% ($100 per year)
- Maturity Date (bond term) = 3 years

So, the question we are answering is how much would we pay today to receive $100 in coupon payments in Year 1, $100 in coupon payments in Year 2, $100 in coupon payments in Year 3, and repayment of the $1,000 principal at the end of Year 3? The cash payments would look as follows:

	Yr 1	Yr 2	Yr 3
Coupon Payments	$100	$100	$100
Principal Payments			$1,000

And the formula to calculate the Present Vale (how much your client would pay today) would look as follows:

$$\text{Price} = \frac{C}{(1+y)^1} + \frac{C}{(1+y)^2} \cdots \frac{C+F}{(1+y)^t}$$

Where:

- "Price" is how much your client would pay today for the bond
- "C" is the Coupon Payments your client will receive
- "F" is the face value of the bond (the principal amount to be repaid)
- "y" is the discount rate used to calculate the present value amount. For purposes of this calculation, we will use a discount rate of 8%
- "t" is the Time or the year that the cash payment will be received

Inputting the numbers, the calculation would look as follows:

$$\text{Price} = \frac{100}{(1+8\%)^1} + \frac{100}{(1+8\%)^2} + \frac{100+1{,}000}{(1+8\%)^3}$$

Your client explains that he and other investors use this calculation to determine how much to pay for a bond today given the bond's face value, the investor's required minimum earnings from the bond as an investment, the bond's coupon payments, and the face value of the bond (the principal amount the investor will be repaid at maturity).

This is a very straight forward time value of money calculation used to determine how much the future stream of cash flows expected to be received in the future is worth in today's dollars. Hopefully, you now have a clearer understanding of how to value debt.

C. Cost of Equity

Similar to a corporation wanting to calculate the cost of debt, a corporation also would want to calculate the cost of its equity. Note, however, that the cost of equity is much less intuitive than the cost of debt. The cost of debt is easy to calculate, but the cost of equity is not as straight-forward.

As an attorney, you might have clients who are corporations seeking investors or you might have clients who are investors seeking to purchase shares in a corporation. Both types of clients have to place a money value on the shares. The corporation must determine how much to sell the shares for, and the investor has to determine how much to pay for the shares. This is the question of determining the cost of equity. There are two perspectives involved in thinking about the cost of equity. The first is from the perspective of the corporation and the second is from the perspective of the investor.

1. Corporation's Perspective

From the corporation's perspective, the corporation will want to know what return the corporation has to offer to entice an investor to purchase the corporation's shares. This is admittedly a very complex concept that we will leave to a more advanced corporate finance course. But we can better understand the concept of the cost of equity by considering it from the investor's perspective as we will do below.

2. Investor's Perspective

From the investor's perspective, investors generally seek the maximum return for an investment while incurring as minimal amount of risk as possible. Accordingly, when determining how and whether to invest capital, an investor is going to consider different investments and the corresponding amounts of risk for those investments. So, when comparing investments, if an investor can invest in another security or investment and receive the same return with a lower risk, broadly speaking, the investor is going to lean toward the investment that provides the lower risk to obtain the similarly higher return. How does this relate to the cost of equity, you might wonder? Well, an investor is going to look at the potential return of an equity investment in a corporation, determine the related riskiness of that investment and compare that risk and return to the risks and return of other investments such as bonds, real estate, or maybe international investments. So, in essence, the corporation's cost of equity is the minimum return that an investor would require to invest in the corporation instead of another investment while comparing the riskiness of those investments.

Legal Highlights

Capital Markets and Valuation

Investors and corporations sometimes purchase shares for reasons other than to earn a profit. Sometimes an investor or a corporation purchase shares in a corporation not to earn money from that investment but to gain a controlling voting interest in that corporation to enable the investor to control or even liquidate the corporation. (This sometimes occurs if the corporation is a corporate competitor. For those of you who just thought, "Wait, antitrust!?!"—good catch.) Shares are also sometimes purchased to enable the investor or corporation to own the corporation's valuable assets like real estate or intellectual property.

---

3. Equity Valuation

Remember that investors will consider the riskiness of an investment when determining the minimum return the investor will require to invest in equity. This means that an investor would require that the rate of return on an equity investment in a corporation must (i) be higher than the risk-free rate, and (ii) offer a higher return than a return on other less risky investments.

Similar to a debt calculation, an investor will calculate the present value of the investor's anticipated future cash flows from an equity investment to determine the financial value of that investment. You may recall those future cash flows for an equity investment will include (i) equity appreciation, (ii) earnings from dividends, and (iii) cash from a corporate liquidation.

Chapter 10 Highlights

- Capital is necessary for the operation of a business. That capital can be obtained via debt or equity, but there is a direct and indirect cost to the corporation to obtain this capital.

- When obtaining debt, a borrower must determine how much interest the borrower is willing to pay for that debt. The interest rate is going to be determined by the amount of principal borrowed, market interest rates and investments, and the lender's risk of being repaid that debt.

- US Treasuries are considered risk-free investments in American finance.

- US Treasuries' rate of return is considered the risk-free rate.

- As the riskiness of an investment increases, the investor will require a higher return.

- Given the fundamental concept of "the higher the risk, the higher the return," investors will require a return higher than the risk-free rate for any investment other than a US Treasury.

- An investor's minimum required return on an equity investment should approximate the return that can be earned on other investments that have similar investment risk.

- While there are many online calculators and websites that will do this calculation for you, the goal for you here is to learn that the financial value of an investment today is broadly, simply speaking, a calculation of how much to pay today for a future stream of cash flows.

- Risk can be quantified to help investors evaluate the minimum return an investor will require for purchasing equity.

That's it! You made it through. Congratulations!

Appendix One

Definitions

Author's note about definitions—these accounting and business concepts are more complicated in practice and have more nuance and caveats than presented here. So, please note that these definitions are for the purposes of providing you a general understanding of the concepts, not an exact definition.

1. **Account**—accounts are the line items that comprise the financial statements. Major accounts include cash, accounts receivable, accounts payable, retained earnings, revenue and depreciation. A list of some of the most common accounts are included in this book for your reference.

2. **Accounts Payable**—found on the Balance Sheet. Accounts payable occur when the corporation purchases inventory on credit. An example of this is when Widget Shoes purchases laces for its shoes from a vendor for $3,000. The vendor expects to be paid, but Widget Shoes promises to pay for the laces within 30 days of receipt of the laces. Once the laces are delivered from the vendor to Widget Shoes, Widget Shoes owes the $3,000 to the vendor. That $3,000 is a liability for Widget Shoes and must be reflected on the Balance Sheet of Widget Shoes. Thus, upon receipt of the laces, Widget Shoes would record $3,000 as accounts payable to record the debt Widget Shoes owes to the vendor.

3. **Accumulated Depreciation**—found on the Balance Sheet. The cumulative depreciation expense over the lifetime of an asset.

4. **Accumulated Amortization**—found on the Balance Sheet. The cumulative amortization expense over the lifetime of an asset.

5. **Additional Paid-in-Capital (APIC)**—found on the Balance Sheet. The difference between a share's par value and the amount for which the corporation sells the share during an offering. For example, if the share's par value is $1 and the corporation sells the share to an investor for $10, then the additional paid-in-capital is $9.

6. **Amortization Expense**—found on the Income Statement. The amount in a fiscal period by which the corporation reduces an intangible asset's book value over the useful life of the asset.

7. **Articles of Incorporation**—the charter of the corporation that must be filed with the state agencies regulating corporations to create the corporation in that state.

8. **Asset**—a thing of value that a corporation owns, or has a right to, that the corporation expects to be able to convert to cash. Found on the Balance Sheet.

9. **Authorized Shares**—the number of shares the corporation is authorized to issue as stated in the corporation's Articles of Incorporation.

10. **Bond**—a type of debt. Bonds are units of a total borrowing from a corporation or government entity. For example, a corporation may wish to borrow $2 million. The corporation may sell units of that $2 million in $1,000 increments to individuals, corporations, or government entities. A bond is often unsecured and must be repaid by a specified date. Found on the Balance Sheet.

11. **Book Value**—the value of an asset as listed in the financial statement.

12. **Borrower**—the entity that borrows cash with an expectation that the cash be repaid.

13. **By-laws**—the internal governing document of a corporation that details how the corporation will govern its internal workings.

14. **Capital**—typically refers to cash that a corporation seeks from equity investors or lenders.

15. **Capitalized Assets**—found on the Balance Sheet. This occurs when a corporation incurs expenses that the corporation chooses not to post to the Income Statement, but instead combines those expenses into a single asset on the Balance Sheet. For example, a corporation might own a truck that has reached the end of its useful life. The truck would then no longer be listed as an asset on the Balance Sheet. If the corporation instead chooses to repair the truck and that repair extends the truck's useful life for another 10 years, the corporation now has a new asset that must be recorded on the Balance Sheet. The cost of that repair would normally be an expense on the Income Statement. Instead, the corporation can instead post that amount as the value of the truck and going forward, list that truck as an asset on the Balance Sheet for the amount of that repair.

16. **Cash**—cash and cash equivalents that are owned by the corporation. Found on the Balance Sheet.

17. **Cash Equivalents**—short term and highly liquid investments that are so liquid they are like cash. Found on the Balance Sheet.

18. **Common Stock**—a type of share in a corporation, as distinguished from preferred stock. Common shareholders have the statutory right to vote for the Board of Directors. The rights of common shareholders are set forth in state statute. Found on the Balance Sheet.

19. **Convertible**—a convertible security is a security that allows the holder to convert that security from one form to another. You frequently see this with

bonds or preferred shares where they allow the holder to convert that bond or preferred share to shares of common stock.

20. **Corporation**—a legal entity that is separate and legally distinct from the shareholders. It is created by drafting and filing Articles of Incorporation with the applicable state agency in a manner set forth in the state's corporation's statute.

21. **Cost of Goods Sold**—found on the Income Statement. It is the cost that the corporation has incurred to acquire, manufacture, and produce its inventory.

22. **Current Assets**—found on the Balance Sheet. These are assets that the corporation expects to convert to cash within the next twelve months.

23. **Current Liabilities**—found on the Balance Sheet. These are liabilities that the corporation expects to have to pay within the next twelve months.

24. **Current Maturities of Long-Term Debt**—a current liability found on the Balance Sheet. It is the portion of the corporation's long-term debt that is due and payable within the next twelve months. For example, assume a corporation is repaying a $100,000 loan over a ten-year period with $10,000 due and payable every year. At the beginning of the first year, $10,000 would be the current maturities of long-term debt, and $90,000 would be long-term debt. At the end of the first year, $10,000 would have been repaid leaving a balance of $90,000, with $10,000 of that due in Year 2 and $80,000 due over the remaining eight years. Thus, at the beginning of the second year, $10,000 would be current maturities of long-term debt, and $80,000 would be long-term debt.

25. **Depreciation Expense**—the amount by which the corporation reduces a tangible asset's book value over the useful life of the asset. Found on the Balance Sheet.

26. **Dividends**—the amount of net profit that the Board of Directors has declared should be returned to the shareholders. Dividends in publicly traded companies are typically declared in payments per share. For example, a corporation might declare a cash dividend of $2.38 per share. Thus, a shareholder would receive $2.38 for each share that the shareholder owns in that corporation.

27. **Equity**—
    - the equity a homeowner has in a house, which is generally defined as the market value of the house minus the amount of debt that the homeowner owes on the house.
    - the amount of equity in a corporation which is loosely considered the amount of assets on a corporation's Balance Sheet less the amount of liabilities on that corporation's Balance Sheet.
    - the amount of capital that an investor is investing in a corporation.

28. **Expenses**—found on the Income Statement. These are the costs that the corporation incurs in operating it business.

29. **Face Value**—
    - the principal amount of a bond.
    - the original principal amount of a promissory note

30. **Fiscal Period**—the period over which financial statements are run. Typically, though not exclusively, companies have fiscal months, fiscal quarters (three months), and fiscal years (twelve months).

31. **Future Value**—time value of money calculation. The value in the future of a current lump sum or current stream of cash flows given a specified rate of return.

32. **Goodwill**—found on Balance Sheet in Long-Term Assets. It is a complicated calculation, but broadly refers to the excess that an acquiring corporation pays to acquire another corporation.

33. **Gross Profit Margin**—a financial ratio calculated from the Income Statement. It is gross profit divided by revenue.

34. **Insolvent**—a corporation is unable to pay its debts as those debts become due.

35. **Interest**—the amount that a lender charges a borrower as a cost of borrowing money.

36. **Interest Rate**—the rate, expressed as a percentage of the principal, that the lender charges a borrower as a cost of borrowing money.

37. **Inventory**—a type of asset found on the Balance Sheet. The items that the corporation sells in its day-to-day operations.

38. **Issued Shares**—shares that are issued or sold by the corporation to shareholders. Issued shares are all of the shares that are issued, including those that have been repurchased by the corporation.

39. **Lender**—an entity who lends money with an expectation of repayment.

40. **Liability**—what a corporation owes to others. Liabilities represent claims on the corporation's assets. Liabilities include current and non-current liabilities. Liabilities include secured and unsecured debt. Found on the Balance Sheet.

41. **Long-Term Debt**—found on the Balance Sheet under liabilities. It is debt that the corporation has incurred that is expected to become due over a period greater than twelve months.

42. **Loans to Owners**—a type of asset found on the Balance Sheet. They are loans that the corporation has made to owners. It is an asset because owners are obligated to repay the loans and thus the corporation has the legal right to receive the loan repayment.

43. **Marketable Securities**—a type of asset found on the Balance Sheet. They are short-term securities that the corporation has purchased. They improve liquidity.

44. **Maturity Date**—the date by when a debt must be repaid.

45. **Net Profit**—also known as Net Income. It is found on the Income Statement. It is the final amount of profit that the corporation has generated over the fiscal period.

46. **Net Profit Margin**—a financial ratio calculated from the Income Statement. It is the net profit divided by revenue.

47. **Non-Current Assets**—found on the Balance Sheet. They are assets that the corporation does not expect to convert to cash within the next twelve months.

48. **Non-Current Liabilities**—found on the Balance Sheet. They are liabilities that the corporation does not expect to have to pay within the next twelve months.

49. **Notes Payable**—found on the Balance Sheet as a short-term liability. They represent short-term debt that the corporation owes.

50. **Operating Expense**—found on the Income Statement. These are expenses that the corporation incurs operating its day-to-day business, such as rent expense, salary expense, or utilities expense.

51. **Operating Profit**—found on the Income Statement. This is the profit that the corporation has generated after accounting for costs of goods sold and operating expenses.

52. **Operating Profit Margin**—a financial ratio calculated from the Income Statement. It is operating profit divided by revenue.

53. **Outstanding Shares**—the number of shares that the corporation has issued or sold and not yet repurchased.

54. **Par Value**—the book value of a share, often listed by publicly traded companies in a fraction of a penny.

55. **Preferred Stock**—a type of share in a corporation, as distinguished from common stock. Preferred stock often has preferences in liquidity, dividend distribution and repayment preference over common shareholders if the corporation is liquidated. The rights of preferred shareholders are set forth in state statutes and in agreements between investors and the companies in which the investor is investing. Found on the Balance Sheet.

56. **Prepayment**—payment of a debt prior to the maturity date.

57. **Present Value**—the time value of money calculation of the value in today's dollars of a future stream of cash flows or a lump sum to be received in the future.

58. **Principal**—the amount of money that a borrower borrows from a lender.

59. **Property, Plant, and Equipment**—types of long-term assets of a corporation. Typically includes assets such as office buildings, warehouses, factories, and heavy equipment and machinery. Found on the Balance Sheet.

60. **Redemption**—repayment of a bond before the maturity date. Some bonds are "callable" which means that the bond can be "called"—meaning prepaid—prior to the maturity date.

61. **Retained Earnings**—found on the Balance Sheet in the shareholder's equity section. Broadly, it is the amount of net profit that the corporation has retained in the corporation.

62. **Revenue**—the amount of income that a corporation has earned over the fiscal period. Revenue does not equal the amount of cash that the corporation has received. Found on the Income Statement.

63. **Salaries Payable**—the amount of salaries expense incurred by the corporation, but not yet paid. Found on the Balance Sheet.

64. **Shares (synonymous with stock)**—the individual units of ownership of a corporation.

65. **Shareholders (synonymous with stockholders)**—the owners of the corporation. Shareholders own shares.

66. **Shareholders' Equity**—assets minus liabilities on the Balance Sheet.

67. **Solvency**—ability of a corporation to pay its debts as they become due.

68. **Stock**—synonymous with shares. See definition for shares above.

69. **Term**—

    - the period of time over which a debt must be repaid.

    - the period of time of a contract.

70. **Term Sheet**—colloquially refers to the document containing the business terms of a transaction that are agreed to before drafting a contract memorializing the transaction.

71. **Treasury Stock**—shares of a corporation that have been issued, subsequently repurchased and belong to the corporation, and have not been cancelled. Treasury stock are shares that are authorized, issued, but no longer outstanding.

72. **Working Capital**—a financial ratio that is a measure of liquidity. Working capital is current assets less current liabilities.

List of Major Financial Statement Accounts

Balance Sheet

Assets
  Accounts Receivable
  Accumulated Amortization
  Accumulated Depreciation
  Cash and Cash Equivalents
  Goodwill
  Intangible Assets (such as IP)
  Inventory
  Investments
  Prepaid Expenses
  Property, Plant and Equipment
    (PP&E)
  Supplies

Liabilities
  Accounts Payable
  Current Maturities of Long-Term
    Debt
  Interest Payable
  Loans Payable
  Long Term Debt
  Rent Payable
  Salaries Payable
  Taxes Payable
  Unearned Revenue

Equity
  Additional Paid-in-Capital
  Common Stock, Preferred Stock and
    Treasury Sock
  Dividends
  Retained Earnings

Income Statement

Revenue
  Revenue

Expenses
  Amortization Expense
  Cost of Goods Sold
  Depreciation Expense
  Interest Expense
  Sales, General and Administrative
    Expenses
  Tax Expense

Profitability
  Net Profit

Index